Michael Slater has written extensively on Dickens and currently edits the four-volume *Uniform Edition of Dickens's Journalism*. He is Professor of Victorian Literature at Birkbeck College, London, a former editor of *The Dickensian* and a past President of the International Dickens Fellowship.

AN INTELLIGENT PERSON'S
GUIDE TO DICKENS

AN
INTELLIGENT
PERSON'S GUIDE
TO
DICKENS

Michael Slater

Duckbacks

First published in 1999 by
Gerald Duckworth & Co. Ltd.
61 Frith Street, London W1D 3JL
Tel: 020 7434 4242
Fax: 020 7434 4420
Email: enquiries@duckworth-publishers.co.uk
www.ducknet.co.uk

Published in 2001 by Duckbacks, a paperback
imprint of Duckworth Media Group

A catalogue record for this book is available
from the British Library

ISBN 0 7156 3088 1

Typeset by Ray Davies
Printed in Great Britain by
BOOKMARQUE Ltd, Croydon, Surrey

Contents

For
Beryl Gray, John Grigg and
Peer Hultberg

Preface

This book is addressed to 'intelligent persons' interested in finding out what Dickens was, and is, about – in both senses of that phrase. During his thirty-five years or so at the top of the literary tree in the English-speaking world (and great fame in most of Europe too) he published fourteen and a half full-length novels, a great deal of shorter fiction – most notably the evergreen *Christmas Carol* – and a mass of sketches, essays, topical journalism and other miscellaneous prose, including travel books about America and Italy and *A Child's History of England*. He also edited weekly journals (even, briefly, a national newspaper), made dozens of eloquent and powerful speeches to a great variety of charitable organisations, and busied himself with an immense amount of other work in this field – including, for many years, actively overseeing the running of a 'Home for Homeless Women'. During the last twelve years of his life he also gave phenomenally successful Public Readings of his own work to enraptured audiences throughout Britain and in the north-eastern United States. These readings were a culmination of his vibrant relationship with the public which he once described as 'personally affectionate and like no other man's'.

In today's jargon all this activity and productivity could be described as having formed Dickens's 'project'. What this little book seeks to do is to give readers some sense of the leading ideas and beliefs, the artistic ideals and ambitions, that largely inspired this Dickensian project and that may be found diffused throughout it – some sense of what we might call 'Dickensian values'. It is not difficult to imagine how comic Dickens would have found our present-day obsession with 'mission state-ments', given his unforgettable satire on mid-Victorian mission-mongers in *Bleak House* (with the hapless Mr Jellyby leaning his despairing head against the wall and adjuring his daughter, 'My child, never have a Mission!'). It has to be said, nevertheless, that what is attempted here can be seen, in part at least, as an attempt to extrapolate the materials for something like a mission statement from the multitudinous and teeming pages of Dickens's oeuvre and from the extensive records of his life.

I should perhaps add that what this book does *not* offer is any kind of detailed survey of Dickens's views and opinions on society, gender issues, politics, crime and punishment, London, America, etc., etc. This would be a work of most egregious supererogation, since there already exists a whole library of excellent books providing ample information about such mat-ters, together with detailed and extensive commentary on them. Rather, I have tried to go behind these topics to focus on the basic beliefs that shaped and informed Dickens's views about them. This book is, therefore, not a sort of potted biography. I do indeed make reference from time to time to certain details of Dickens's life but I am not primarily concerned with the events of his personal, professional or public life, or with what his longtime friend and greatest biographer John Forster calls his 'hard experiences in boyhood', with his domestic relationships, his dealings with publishers and illustrators – nor even with that subject of apparently endless media fascination, the question of what he did or did not get up to in his later years with that long since exceedingly 'visible woman' Nelly Ternan. Again, there is a wealth of extremely well-researched Dickens biographies and biographical studies that, although now costing rather more than Auden's 'shilling life', will certainly 'give you all the facts' – and plenty of surmises into the bargain.

This is emphatically not a book addressed to Dickens spe-cialists, amateur or professional, but to those 'general readers' (for many years now a threatened species but happily not yet extinct) who – whether they have read very little Dickens, or whether they have, in the words of that eminent literary character ('*with* a wooden leg'), Silas Wegg in *Our Mutual Friend*, 'been slap-bang through him' – may have become interested in trying to trace the main ideas and beliefs that motivated him – or (to substitute an expressive American idiom for a worn-out English metaphor) to find out 'where he was coming from'.

In one of his American speeches in 1842, Dickens expressed his belief that 'a reader will rise from the perusal of a book with some defined and tangible idea of the writer's moral creed and broad purposes if he has any at all', and it is to help bring such an idea as regards Dickens himself (which may not always be so 'defined and tangible' for modern non-specialist readers) into clearer focus that I have written this book. It would, of course, be the height of 'imbecility' (to borrow one of his favourite terms of disapprobation) for any commentator to claim that he or she has neatly summed up Dickens's 'moral creed and broad purposes' – has, as it were, plucked out the heart of his mystery, in 45,000 words (or in 450,000, for that matter). I seek merely to provide a few signposts for those who want to get some overall sense of the main concepts and beliefs in the light of which Dickens wrote all his work and managed his professional life generally. And I naturally hope that such signposting will help in some degree to enhance the reader's understanding and enjoyment of that dazzling and haunting stream of stories, essays and journalism that flowed for thirty-six years of the last century and that we know as 'Dickens', the stream that began with, in Forster's phrase, 'the first sprightly runnings of his genius' in *Sketches by Boz*, and that vanished so untimely leaving a last half-told tale, dealing with murder (or was it just attempted murder?) in the shadow of a cathedral.

Michael Slater

Fancy

'So you would carpet your room ... with repre-
sentations of flowers, would you?' said the gentleman.
'Why would you?'

'If you please, Sir, I am very fond of flowers,' returned
the girl.

'And that is why you would put tables and chairs upon
them, and have people walking over them with heavy
boots?'

'It wouldn't hurt them, Sir. They wouldn't crush or
wither ... and I would fancy —'

'Ay, ay, ay! But you mustn't fancy,' cried the gentleman, quite elated by coming so happily to his point.
'That's it! You are never to fancy.'

'You are not, Cecilia Jupe,' Thomas Gradgrind solemnly repeated, 'to do anything of that kind'.

(*Hard Times*, Book I, ch. 2)

By Dickens's day, no doubt partly as a result of Coleridge's
famous distinction between the two words in chapter 13 of his
Biographia Literaria (1817), the word 'fancy' had ceased to be
virtually synonymous with 'imagination' and was generally
used to denote an inferior form of that faculty. Through its
exercise – and by means of such literary figures as allusion,
simile and metaphor – a writer could achieve decorative or,
maybe, wittily satirical effects, a sort of verbal equivalent of
rococo in art. For Dickens, however, the terms 'fancy' and
'fanciful' always remained words of great power, and through-

out his career he used them interchangeably with 'imagination' and 'imaginative'. In a fine essay on the topic Philip Collins once observed, ' "Fancy" is, perhaps, Dickens's favourite abstraction, and the one which can take us furthest into his "philosophy" ' (*ES*, 1961). Dickens himself once characterised his artistry as that of 'a fanciful photographer', someone who gives an exact description of what he observes, but who also re-creates it for the reader, makes it memorable and meaningful through his imaginative treatment of what he sees. And Dickens, with what his great actor friend Macready called his 'clutching eye', was an observer *par excellence*.

In a letter to W. H. Wills, his sub-editor on *Household Words*, from the north of England during his first Public Readings tour, Dickens wrote:

> I walked from Durham to Sunderland [a mere 13 miles, only a mile longer than Dickens's normal daily walk], and made a little fanciful photograph in my mind of Pit-Country, which will come well into *H. W.* one day. I couldn't help looking upon my mind as I was doing it, as a sort of capitally prepared and highly sensitive plate. And I said, without the least conceit … 'it really is a pleasure to work with you, you receive the impression so nicely'. (24 Sept. 1858)

We might juxtapose with this a quotation from another letter, one that was included by Forster in his biography, in which Dickens says:

> It does not seem to me to be enough to say of any description that it is the exact truth. The exact truth must be there; but the merit or art in the narrator, is the manner of stating the truth. As to which thing in literature, it always seems to me that there is a world to be done. And in these times, when the tendency is to be frightfully

literal and catalogue-like – to make the thing, in short, a
sort of sum in reduction that any miserable creature can
do in that way – I have an idea (really founded on the love
of what I profess), that the very holding of popular literature through a kind of popular dark age, may depend on
such fanciful treatment. (Forster, IX.1)

We shall return later to the idea of a popular dark age that
Dickens expresses in the last sentence. As to 'fanciful treatment' itself, anyone who has read any Dickens at all will hardly
need reminding that this is as much his literary hallmark as the
'Metaphysical' conceit is John Donne's. It can be seen in all his
writings – especially, of course, in his novels, from the moment
in *Pickwick Papers* when, at the beginning of Chapter 2, 'that
punctual servant of all work', the sun, rises and begins 'to strike
a light' and Mr Pickwick 'bursts like another sun from his
slumbers', right through to almost the very last paragraph
Dickens ever wrote in which he describes 'flecks of brightness'
darting into the 'sternest marble corners' of Cloisterham Cathedral and 'fluttering there like wings'.

The most famous and comprehensive example of this central
– and, to him, supremely important – quality of Dickens's art is
his depiction of London. This was as celebrated in his own day
as in ours (we might recall Walter Bagehot's famous phrase
about Dickens describing the city, 'like a special correspondent
for posterity'), and it has been profoundly influential in shaping
all later generations' conception of Victorian London. From the
streets and neighbourhoods of *Sketches by Boz*, teeming with
vivid, frequently grotesque, forms of human existence, and the
sinister labyrinth of Fagin's London in *Oliver Twist* to the
fog-bound, muddy metropolis of *Bleak House* and the darkly
brooding or 'black, shrill' city of *Our Mutual Friend*, 'Dickens's
London' has etched itself on the national consciousness –
indeed, one might say, in view of the constant stream of over-
seas visitors who come in quest of it, on global consciousness.

This is the city presented under so many startlingly strange aspects by the 'Uncommercial Traveller', the persona Dickens adopted for most of his journalistic writings in the 1860s. (Introducing himself, the Traveller tells us that he travels 'for the great house of Human Interest Brothers' and has 'rather a large connection in the fancy goods way'.)

Here is a brief example of Dickens 're-creating' London, taken from 'Night Walks', one of the most powerful of the 'Uncommercial' essays. He is wandering the city in the small hours of a night in March, 'Houselessness' incarnate, and finds himself on Waterloo Bridge, notorious for the number of people who killed themselves by jumping from it into the Thames:

> ... the river had an awful look, the buildings on the bank were muffled in black shrouds, and the reflected lights seemed to originate deep in the water, as if the spectres of suicides were holding them to show where they went down. The wild moon and clouds were as restless as an evil conscience in a tumbled bed, and the very shadow of the immensity of London seemed to lie oppressively on the river.

The astonishing, macabre 'fancy' shown in this description makes it unforgettable and we may presume that Dickens took as much artistic pride in it as he had taken in a somewhat similar, and no less arresting, fancy, 'the fruit ... of a solitary walk by starlight on the cliffs' near Broadstairs twenty years before, when he was writing *The Old Curiosity Shop* and described Little Nell contemplating the stars reflected in a river

> ... shining in the same majestic order as when the dove beheld them gleaming through the swollen waters, upon the mountain tops down far below, and dead mankind, a million fathoms deep. (*OCS*, 42)

Dickens told Forster that he thought the image of dead mankind a million fathoms deep 'the best thing in the sentence': 'I have a notion of the dreadful silence down there, and of the stars shining down upon their drowned eyes' (4 Oct. 1840).

This last example with its allusion to the story of Noah's Flood points us towards a key aspect of the 'fanciful' in Dickens, namely the frequency with which it draws on, and refers to, legends, fairy-tales, folklore and popular literature generally, especially those stories so passionately read and re-read by him as a child and loved by him all his life. These stories include, in particular, 'Bluebeard' (somewhat disturbingly, we find Dickens alluding to this story more frequently, probably, than to any other fairy tale), 'The Sleeping Beauty' and 'Jack the Giant Killer', and legends like those of Dick Whittington or Robin Hood, or literature like Cervantes's *Don Quixote*, *The Pilgrim's Progress*, *Robinson Crusoe*, the novels of Le Sage, Fielding, Smollett and Sterne, Goldsmith's *Vicar of Wakefield*, *The Tales of the Genii*, and above all 'that mighty talisman' as he once called it, *The Arabian Nights*. Again and again, we find Dickens invoking these beloved texts both in his fiction and non-fictional writings, sometimes playfully, sometimes with more serious intent. Equally important to him in this respect were Shakespeare's plays, first experienced in Rochester, the 'birthplace of his fancy' as Forster calls it, in the thrilling intimacy of the little theatre there.

> Richard the Third, in a very uncomfortable cloak, had first appeared to me there and had made my heart leap by backing up against the stage-box in which I was posted, while struggling for life against the virtuous Richmond' (*UT*, 'Dullborough Town')

While it is true to say that the novels of most of the great Victorian writers tend often to make allusions to fairy tales, as likewise to *The Pilgrim's Progress*, *The Arabian Nights*, and

Shakespeare, it is certainly also the case that none of them does so to the degree, and with the purposefulness, that Dickens does. The relevant biographical facts are well known. During his rather solitary childhood, and the miserable days that followed the family's move to London amidst increasing financial difficulties, little Charles was comforted and sustained by reading, re-reading, and acting out characters from some of the books mentioned in the previous paragraph, copies of which (published in a cheap reprint series) his father happened to own. 'They were', says Forster, 'a host of friends when he had no single friend'. What Dickens himself stresses in his transposition of these early experiences into his quasi-autobiographical novel *David Copperfield* is that the stories 'kept alive [his] fancy and [his]hope of something beyond that time and place'; they were his lifeline to the future and nourished in him that quality which was to bring him fame, wealth and the devoted love of countless thousands, his extraordinary imagination.

It is hardly surprising that Dickens came to make so close a connection between the healthy development of any child and that child's exposure to stories and imaginative literature generally. His novels offer many examples of childhood stunted or perverted by the denial of such mental nourishment which was, he argued in one of his journalistic essays, at the same time an education in morality:

We may assume that we are not singular in entertaining a very great tenderness for the fairy literature of our childhood. What enchanted us then, and is captivating a million of young fancies now, has, at the same blessed time of life, enchanted vast hosts of men and women who have done their long day's work, and laid their grey heads down to rest. It would be hard to estimate the amount of gentleness and mercy that has made its way among us through these slight channels. Forbearance, courtesy, consideration for the poor and aged, kind treatment of

animals, the love of nature, abhorrence of tyranny and
brute force – many such good things have been first
nourished in the child's heart by this powerful aid.
('Frauds on the Fairies', *HW*, 1 Oct. 1853)

Louisa and Tom Gradgrind in *Hard Times*, whose relent-
lessly factual education leads one to the brink of adultery and
the other into downright criminality, clearly represent Dickens's
starkest, most schematic, presentation of childhood betrayed;
and their obsessed father's prize pupil, Bitzer, most effectively
dramatises Dickens's horror at the kind of school 'where the
bright childish imagination is utterly discouraged' and where,
he declared, addressing a dinner of the Warehousemen and
Clerks' Schools Association in 1857, 'I have never seen among
the pupils, whether boys or girls, anything but little parrots and
small calculating machines'.

Other examples of this deformation of children are the
grotesque Smallweed clan in *Bleak House* (the family, having
'discountenanced all story-books, fairy-tales, fictions, and
fables, … has had no child born to it, and … the complete little
men and women whom it has produced, have been observed to
bear a resemblance to old monkeys with something depressing
on their minds'). Or, for a more psychologically rendered
portrait, there is Arthur Clennam, the wan hero of *Little Dorrit*,
'only child of parents who weighed, measured and priced
everything' and in whose young life there was 'nothing graceful or gentle anywhere' until he saw pretty young Flora Casby,
the 'first face that had soared out of his gloomy life into the
bright glories of fancy'. Nature itself had to nourish the imagination that had been well nigh starved to death in Arthur's early
childhood with such potentially disastrous results for his moral
growth:

At no Mother's knee but hers [nature's], had he ever
dwelt in his youth on hopeful promises, on playful fan-

cies, on the harvests of tenderness and humility that lie hidden in the early-fostered seeds of the imagination; on the oaks of retreat from blighting winds, that have the germs of their strong roots in nursery acorns. (*LD*, II. 34)

In the Dickensian value-system 'wonder' is closely linked with 'Fancy'. In a review of a book called *The Poetry of Science* that he wrote anonymously for *The Examiner* in 1848 Dickens praised the author, Robert Hunt, Keeper of Mining Records at the Museum of Practical Geology, for the 'striking and good' design of his book:

To show that the facts of science are at least as full of poetry, as the most poetical fancies ever founded on an imperfect observation and a distant suspicion of them (as, for example, among the ancient Greeks); to show that if the Dryades no longer haunt the woods, there is, in every forest, in every tree, in every leaf, and in every ring on every sturdy trunk, a beautiful and wonderful creation, always changing, always going on, always bearing testimony to the stupendous workings of Almighty Wisdom, and always leading the student's mind from wonder to wonder, until he is wrapt and lost in the vast worlds of wonder by which he is surrounded from his cradle to his grave; it is a purpose worthy of the natural philosopher, and salutary to the spirit of the age.

Scientific discoveries, far from binding us 'in stern utilitarian chains' like the poor Gradgrind children with their 'little conchological cabinet, and ... little metallurgical cabinet, and ... little mineralogical cabinet' with the 'specimens ... all arranged and labelled' (*HT*, I. 3), should, in fact, become the successors to the fairy-tales of our early reading.

As fairy stories develop our moral senses, so these will develop our spiritual ones by finding just as great and imagination-stimulating wonders in the 'real' world of geology, physics, palaeontology, astronomy, etc.

> Caverns in rocks, choked with rich treasures shut up from all but the enchanted hand, Science has blown to atoms; as she can rend and rive the rocks themselves; but in those rocks she has found, and read aloud, the great stone book which is the history of the earth itself, even when darkness sat upon the face of the deep ... . From within them she has brought the bones, and pieced together the skeletons, of monsters that would have crushed the noted dragons of the fables at a blow.

Such knowledge, besides revealing ever more of the infinite power and infinite complexity of the work of that 'Creator' whom Darwin was to invoke so memorably at the end of his *Origin of Species*, can also magically transform our perception of the everyday. It may give a rich strangeness even to our experience of a horrible November day in London as in the famous opening of *Bleak House* in which Dickens deftly combines (as he does in the passage just quoted) Biblical legend and what poor Mrs Gradgrind would call an 'Ology' and depicts a world of mud looking 'as if the waters had but newly retired from the face of the earth, and it would not be wonderful to meet a Megalosaurus, forty feet long or so, waddling like an elephantine lizard up Holborn Hill'. The adult student learning more and more about the earth's history and its material properties, may become 'wrapt and lost in the vast worlds of wonder by which he is surrounded' but children – at least those who are allowed to have a childhood of the mind as well as of the body – will also have intimations of the divine through 'wondering' at the glories of the natural world (Dickens's version of that Wordsworthian 'hour / Of splendour in the grass, of glory in the flower') as expressed in the following quasi-autobiographical passage:

There was once a child, and he strolled about a good deal, and thought of a number of things. He had a sister, who was a child too, and his constant companion. These two used to wonder all day long. They wondered at the beauty of the flowers; they wondered at the height and blueness of the sky; they wondered at the depth of the bright water; they wondered at the goodness and power of GOD who made the lovely world. ('A Child's Dream of a Star', *HW*, 6 April 1850)

*

Little Paul Dombey, listening on the seashore to the waves' intimations of mortality and of immortality, is Dickens's most famous wondering-child figure; his imagination is richly fed by the tales of his attendant, old Glubb, who

'… knows all about the deep sea, and the fish that are in it, and the great monsters that come and lie on rocks in the sun, and dive into the water again when they're startled, blowing and splashing so, that they can be heard for miles.' (*DS*, 12)

Struggling beneath his crushing load of arid academic task work in Dr Blimber's 'little Portico', Paul ventures to tell the Doctor's learned daughter that he thinks he might do better if he could sometimes be allowed to see old Glubb again but is sharply snubbed. 'This', she very truthfully declares, 'is not the place for Glubbs of any kind'. The reader is left in little doubt that the stifling of his 'fancy' was one of the main causes of Paul's early death but, as if in compensation for this, Dickens gives him a recurring deathbed vision of Nature shining with spiritual meaning to ease him into the next world: 'How fast the river runs, between its green banks and the rushes, Floy! But it's very near the sea. I hear the waves! …'

Paul's fascination with the stories of old Glubb, like that of young Walter Gay in the same novel with stories of famous shipwrecks, voyages and perilous travels into distant, 'savage' lands, connects with one abiding source of delighted fancy for Dickens. In his childhood he had had, he wrote, 'a greedy relish' for books of voyages and travels. So strong was his life-long addiction to them – he seemed to have had as many in his library as his beloved Don Quixote had books of chivalry – that he once expressed comic surprise that he had never actually 'been round the world, ... been shipwrecked, ice-environed, tomahawked, or eaten' ('The Long Voyage', *HW*, 31 Dec. 1853).

In fact, Dickens was a classic arm-chair traveller, apart from his American forays and those to France, Italy and Switzerland, all of which were motivated as much by economic considerations as by anything else – though he certainly came to love what he called the 'dear old France of my affections' and to have an often-renewed delight in Paris as the brilliant, sparkling Other of sombre London. Dickens's passion for stories of perils by land and sea seems, in the final analysis, to have been more a matter of national, even racial, pride, 'wondering' at the heroism and endurance of British travellers rather than at anything that might be discovered in the exotic lands into which they penetrated, such lands themselves being more often than not rendered in terms of quasi-Gothic horror.

Bruce is caged in Abyssinia, surrounded by the gory horrors which shall often startle him out of his sleep at home when years have passed away. Franklin, come to the end of his unhappy overland [Arctic] journey ... lies perishing of hunger with his brave companions; each emaciated figure stretched upon its miserable bed without the power to rise: all, dividing the weary days between their prayers, their remembrances of the dear ones at home, and the conversation on the pleasures of

eating .... All the African travellers, wayworn, solitary
and sad, submit themselves ... to drunken, murderous,
man-selling despots of the lowest order of humanity ....
('The Long Voyage')

We never find Dickens presenting real-life distant and alien
cultures, whether 'savage' or 'civilised', as a source of fancy in
themselves. All that he can see in the rituals performed by the
Zulu warriors on show in London is 'a general stamping,
ramping, and raving, remarkable (as everything in savage life
is) for its dire uniformity' ('The Noble Savage', *HW*, 11 June
1853). The equally alien 'civilisation' of the Celestial Empire,
on the other hand, can at least be made to supply wonderfully
zany comedy in Flora Finching's distracted questioning of
Arthur Clennam:

> ... oh do tell me something about the Chinese ladies
> whether their eyes are really so long and narrow always
> putting me in mind of mother-of-pearl fish at cards and
> do they really wear tails down their back and plaited too
> or is it only the men, and when they pull their hair so very
> tight off their foreheads don't they hurt themselves, and
> why do they stick little bells all over their bridge and
> temples and hats and things or don't they really do it?
> (*LD* I. 13)

Generally, however, Dickens is more concerned to bring the
exotic and the fabulous to bear on mundane, everyday life in
19th-century England. He may use the exotic for satirical purposes as when, having inspected a fragment of genuine Chinese
culture that turned up in 1846 at the London docks in the shape
of the junk *Keying*, he transforms it into a device for making
ironic reference to contemporary controversies about ritual in
the Church of England. The crew of the *Keying* had apparently
refused to join the ship until

... a considerable amount of silvered paper, tinfoil, and joss-sticks had been laid in by the owners, for the purposes of their worship; but OUR seamen – far less our bishops, priests, and deacons – never stand out upon points of silvered paper and tin-foil, or the lighting up of joss-sticks upon altars! Christianity is not Chin-Teeism; and therein all insignificant quarrels as to means, are lost sight of in remembrance of the end.

Hard Times represents Dickens's most extensive use of the exotic, real or imagined, for the purposes of satire, beginning, as it does with the schoolmaster M'Choakumchild going to work 'not unlike Morgiana in the Forty Thieves', filling to the brim the little human pitchers before him from the 'boiling store' of his factual knowledge. The great apostle of Fact is subverted by being soon as a figure out of The Arabian Nights. Like his great contemporary fellow-masters of the Grotesque, Carlyle and Browning, Dickens wants to make people see that, as Carlyle put it, their 'very coats and breeches are miracles', to make them, in other words, have life more abundantly.

Dickens never forgot how as a child *The Arabian Nights* had so magically transformed the commonplace for him:

Oh, now all common things become uncommon and enchanted to me. All lamps are wonderful; all rings are talismans. Common flower-pots are full of treasure, with a little earth scattered on the top; trees are for Ali Baba to hide in; beefsteaks are to throw down into the Valley of Diamonds, that the precious stones may stick to them, and be carried by the eagles to their nests, whence the traders, with loud cries, will scare them. Tarts are made, according to the recipe of the Vizier's son of Bussorah, who turned pastrycook after he was set down in his drawers at the gate of Damascus; cobblers are all Mustaphas, and in the habit of sewing up people cut into four pieces, to whom they are taken blindfold. ('A Christmas Tree' *HW*, 21 Dec. 1850)

In one of the last journalistic essays he wrote, 'Mr Barlow' (*ATYR*, 16 Jan. 1869), he deplores the kind of teacher who, like Mr Barlow in Thomas Day's *Sandford and Merton* (1783 – 89), works to dissipate childhood wonder by scientific explanation:

> ... he was always hinting doubts of the veracity of Sind-bad the Sailor. If he could have got hold of the Wonderful Lamp, I knew he would have trimmed it and lighted it, and delivered a lecture over it on the qualities of sperm-oil, with a glance at the whale-fisheries .... He would have caused that hypocritical young prig Harry [Sand-ford] to make an experiment, – with the aid of a temporary building in the garden and a dummy, – dem-onstrating that you couldn't let a choked hunchback down an Eastern chimney with a cord, and leave him upright on the hearth to terrify the Sultan's purveyor.

Throughout all his work, the ability still to delight in *The Arabian Nights* is a sign of virtue. We know that Scrooge's reformation is well under way when he remembers 'dear old honest Ali Baba' and 'the Sultan's Groom turned upside down by the Genii'. The moral gulf between Tom Pinch and his arch-hypocrite of an employer, Mr Pecksniff, is signalled, among other things, by the absurd error Pecksniff makes when referring to the *Nights*:

> '... Unlike the young man in the Eastern tale – who is described as a one-eyed almanack, if I am not mistaken, Mr Pinch?'
> 'A one-eyed calendar, I think, sir,' faltered Tom.
> 'They are pretty nearly the same thing, I believe,' said Mr

Pecksniff, smiling compassionately; 'or they used to be in my time.' (*MC*. 6)

Similarly, whenever Dickens wishes to throw a glowing sense of delighted wonder around some scene of everyday life, he will tend to invoke the *Nights*. The situation of David Copperfield's much-loved friend Tommy Traddles, ensconced in his Gray's Inn chambers 'among the dry law-stationers and the attorneys' offices' with his pretty young wife and her sisters, seems to David 'almost as pleasantly fanciful' as if he had dreamed 'that the Sultan's famous family had been admitted on the roll of attorneys, and had brought the talking bird, the singing tree, and the golden water into Gray's Inn Hall' (*DC*, 59). Only in his very strange last novel, the half-finished *Edwin Drood*, is *Arabian Nights* imagery associated with evil, in the drugged and murderous dreams of Jasper, the cathedral choir-master.

Dickens strongly believed that Fancy had the power to compensate for disappointment in life, loneliness and failure and he dramatises this belief most clearly in one of his Christmas Stories, 'The Poor Relation's Story' (1852), which contains a distinct echo of Lamb's essay 'Dream Children'. Michael, the Poor Relation in the family Christmas circle, acknowledges that to all outward appearances he must appear to be

... rather put upon and disappointed, in a general way ... a bachelor of between fifty-nine and sixty years of age, living on a limited income in the form of a quarterly allowance ... lodging in the Clapham Road — a very clean back room ...

In the 'Castle' of his imagination, however, he lives happily in his 'very comfortable' house ('quite a picture of Home') with his 'dearest and most devoted wife', surrounded by loving children and grandchildren, all the failures of love and the betrayals that he has experienced in real life having been transformed into their opposites; and it is during Christmas and New Year that he spends most time in his imaginary castle 'for the associations of the season seem to hold me there, and the precepts of the season seem to teach me that it is well to be there'.

A sumptuously comic variation on the theme of the compensating imagination is provided by Mrs Gamp, the drunken old midwife in *Martin Chuzzlewit*. She invents with a wealth of wonderful detail (what Henry James calls 'solidity of specification') an infinitely admiring friend Mrs Harris, 'created for the express purpose of holding visionary dialogues with her on all manner of subjects, and invariably winding up with a compliment to the excellence of her nature' (*MC*, 25); indeed, Mrs Gamp's prodigiously fertile fancy can endow Mrs Harris with a whole tribe of relations, each with his or her particular history and distinguishing features. And no matter how basely Mrs Gamp may be betrayed by that 'bage creetur', her faithless business partner Betsey Prig, she still has the devoted love of the Harris family to support her, including little Tommy Harris

> ... as calls me his own Gammy, and truly calls, for bless the little mottled legs of that there precious child (like Canterbury Brawn his own dear father says, which so they are) his own I have been, ever since I found him ... with his small red worsted shoe a-gurglin' in his throat where he had put it in his play, a chick, while they was leavin' of him on the floor a-lookin' for it through the ouse and him a-choakin' sweetly in the parlour!' (*MC*, 49)

Besides assuaging loneliness, fancy can also serve as a powerful private counterbalance to a bleakly 'factual' public life as in the case of Wemmick in *Great Expectations* who is

kept human by being able to return each evening from the
sordid realities and 'Newgate cobwebs' of Jaggers's office in
Little Britain to his 'Aged P. ' ensconced in Wemmick's
little 'Castle' in Walworth with its miniature but imagination-
satisfying fortifications, drawbridge and cannon. Omnipresent
in Dickens's work, in fact, is the idea that Fancy can actually
transform dreary and mundane, even painful or depressing,
reality, into something rich and strange. Mr Micawber is perhaps the supreme example here.

As J.B. Priestley once finely put it:

> If a man who has just been quarrelling with the turncock
> from the waterworks can dismiss the matter with a refer-
> ence to the 'momentary laceration of a wounded spirit,
> made sensitive by a recent collision with the Minion of
> Power', he is beyond the corroding touch of bitter cir-
> cumstance ... his imagination has provided him with one
> of those fairy cloaks that enable their wearers to brave all
> dangers. (*The English Comic Characters*, 1925)

But the idea surely finds its most engaging expression (not
surprisingly) in that most fairy-tale-like of all his novels, *The
Old Curiosity Shop*. Dick Swiveller, who, in some respects at
least, is clearly a projection of Dickens himself ('Dick' was one
of his nicknames for himself), constructs an elaborate benign
fantasy around the person and situation of the brutally abused
child-servant whom he finds imprisoned at the Brasses' house.
Re-naming her 'the Marchioness', he makes believe that the
squalid back-kitchen in which he teaches her to play cards is a
marble-floored palace and takes to addressing her as though she
were an elegant young lady. In due course, and as a direct result
of his behaviour towards her and her response to him, including
saving his life, this is exactly what she does become (splendidly
re-named again by Dick as 'Sophronia Sphynx' though 'to [his]
honour ... he called her the Marchioness from first to last').

Another example might be Captain Cuttle in *Dombey and Son* who delights in imagining a Dick Whittington fortune for his beloved young protégé Walter Gay despite all the evidence of Mr Dombey's hostility to the boy, and who lives to see it all come true (Walter does not, admittedly, actually become Lord Mayor of London – an office that Dickens tends always to treat with ridicule – but he does indeed marry his master's daughter and does become a great City merchant).

Dick Swiveller and Captain Cuttle are perhaps Dickens's greatest practitioners of benign Fancy. There are plenty of malign fanciers, those whose imaginations are perverted by egotism, hypocrisy, hatred of others, greed, jealousy and other such negative emotions, and it is notable that, with the important exception of Skimpole (see below), Dickens makes their self-deserving fancies derive from his beloved Fairy-tales and legends. Such characters may invoke grotesque versions of the pastoral as when the Hon. Mrs Skewton asserts that Nature intended her for 'an Arcadian' and professes a wish to 'retreat to a Swiss farm, and live entirely surrounded by cows – and china' (*DS*, 21), or the exotic as when chilly-bosomed Mrs Merdle expresses herself 'charmed' at the idea of being a 'Savage in the Tropical seas' ('most delightful life and perfect climate I am told'; *LD*, I. 20), but neither Classical literature nor, as we have seen, exotic lands in themselves meant much to Dickens's imagination. Generally, his 'malign fanciers', so to call them, like Bounderby in *Hard Times*, or Silas Wegg in *Our Mutual Friend*, simply re-arrange factual reality, past or present, to suit their own egotistical purposes without any invocation of literary sources (Wegg's 'dropping into poetry' with bizarrely mangled quotations from his stock of street-ballads is simply meant to dazzle Mr Boffin and make him feel particularly obligated). Mrs Sparsit goes further than this in her 'Staircase' fancy but, inspired as it is by vindictive fury towards Louisa Gradgrind for being the unwitting spoiler of her matrimonial schemes, it is more like the casting of an evil spell than a flight of genuine fancy:

> Mrs Sparsit was not a poetical woman; but she took an idea in the nature of an allegorical fancy, into her head. Much watching of Louisa … must have given her as it were a lift, in the way of inspiration. She erected in her mind a mighty Staircase, with a dark pit of shame and ruin at the bottom; and down those stairs, from day to day and hour to hour, she saw Louisa coming. (*HT*, II.10)

The evil spell proves ineffectual in the end, however, as Louisa retreats from the last step. Meanwhile there is a satisfying symmetry about the fact that the two 'malign fanciers' in *Hard Times*, Bounderby and Mrs Sparsit, become the instruments of punishment for each other with Mrs Sparsit unintentionally exploding in a very public way Bounderby's boastful legend about being a self-made man who had been 'born in a ditch', and him driving her away to live in 'a mean little airless lodging' with her relative, the bedridden 'peevish, tormenting Lady Scadgers'.

There is, however, one bad — or rather false — fancier in Dickens who is in a class of his own and who is painted at full length in *Bleak House*. This is the phoney innocent, Harold Skimpole, to be discussed more fully in the next chapter. Skimpole is Fancy's Traitor, manipulating the faculty of imagination for sordid ends. At the opposite end of the spectrum to him stand those whom Fancy dominates to such an extent that they are severed from reality — in other words, the mad. Setting aside an early exercise in Gothic horror, 'A Madman's Manuscript', interpolated into *The Pickwick Papers*, the mad characters in Dickens seem to divide into benign and malign fanciers very much according to the kind of person they were before some great distress or shock drove them mad. Mr Dick in *David Copperfield* in his benevolence towards the young David and Miss Flite in *Bleak House*, promising to 'confer estates' on the Wards in Jarndyce when she gets her judgement 'on the Day of Judgement', are clearly benign. The Gentleman in Small Clothes, on the other hand, who, while he had his wits, was 'the cruellest, wickedest, out-and-outerest old flint that ever drawed breath', makes grotesquely libidinous overtures to poor Mrs Nickleby and later to Miss La Creevy ('Queen of my soul, this goblet sip!', etc.; *NN*, 41). These very funny scenes are in farcical mode, of course, and very much side-shows in a ramblingly episodic novel but later, in *Great Expectations*, Dickens, working in the melodramatic mode, depicts the ghastly, witch-like figure of the jilted Miss Havisham. This malign fancier *par excellence* was originally a spoiled and haughty young heiress who now, with 'her wasting hands' is moulding young Estella's life, seeking to use her to wreak a grotesque vengeance on the whole male sex.

In his one depiction of a major character mentally afflicted from birth, Dickens presents him as having been driven mad in the womb (by his mother's horror at an atrocious double murder committed by her husband); with no life before becoming mad, Barnaby Rudge is neither a benign nor a malign fancier but more like a kind of Gothicised version of Wordsworth's *Idiot Boy*. Wholly mastered by Fancy, he is unable to channel and direct its activity but revels in it, like an out-of-control version of Dickens the artist himself:

'Look down there,' he said softly; 'do you mark how they whisper in each other's ears; then dance and leap, to make believe they are in sport? Do you see how they stop for a moment, when they think there is no one looking, and mutter among themselves again; and then how they roll and gambol, delighted with the mischief they've been plotting ... what is it that they plot and hatch? Do you know?'
'They are only clothes,' returned the guest, 'such as we

wear; hanging on those lines to dry, and fluttering in the wind.'

'Clothes!' echoed Barnaby, …'Ha, ha! Why, how much better to be silly than as wise as you! You don't see shadowy people there, like those that live in sleep – not you. Nor eyes in the knotted panes of glass … I lead a merrier life than you, with all your cleverness . … I'll not change with you, clever as you are, – not I!'

With that he waved his hat above his head, and darted off. 'A strange creature, upon my word!' said the guest … .

'He wants imagination', said Mr Willett, very slowly, and after a long silence; 'that's what he wants' … (*BR*, 10)

Barnaby's imagination is as uncontrolled as a dreamer's – for him, indeed, there is no distinction, as there so sharply is for us, between what he sees in dream and what he sees in reality. Asleep, we are all like him and 'in the quiet hours of the night, one house shuts in as many incoherent and incongruous fancies as a madman's head' (*MC*, ch.5). In one of his 'Night Walks' Dickens pauses outside the walls of the Bedlam lunatic asylum to muse :

Are not all of us outside this hospital, who dream, more or less in the condition of those inside it, every night of our lives? Are we not nightly persuaded, as they daily are, that we associate preposterously with kings and queens, emperors and empresses, and notabilities of all sorts? … I wonder that the great master who knew everything, when he called Sleep the death of each day's life, did not call Dreams the insanity of each day's sanity. (*UT*, 'Night Walks')

In the pre-Freudian way of his day Dickens would have distinguished between simply 'mad' dreams like these in which Fancy has become merely fantastic, altogether divorced from reality, and others, prophetic or visionary, in which the imagination creates allegorical or symbolical scenes expressive of the dreamer's deepest concerns, fears, anxieties, and so on. Such dreams have, of course, always been a great stand-by for poets, dramatists and novelists – as a device for raising narrative tension, for example, or for exploring a character's inner life and emotions, and it is hardly surprising to find Dickens also using them in this way, e.g., the nightmares of Tigg Montague and Jonas Chuzzlewit (*MC*, 42 and 47) and the delirious dreams of fever-stricken Esther Summerson in *Bleak House* (35) and Pip in *Great Expectations* (47). And in his own life there was the celebrated instance of his dream in Genoa in 1844 in which it seemed that the spirit of his idolised dead young sister-in-law, Mary Hogarth, appeared to him and responded to his urgent questioning as to which was the true religion (see below, p. 162); Dickens was evidently very interested in tracing the various raw materials of waking experience on which his imagination had worked to create this scene.

*

In a deceptively off-hand-seeming remark at the end of his preface to what most critics regard as his supreme achievement in fiction Dickens says, 'In *Bleak House*, I have purposely dwelt upon the romantic side of familiar things'. He echoes here a phrase he had used three years earlier, in his 'Preliminary Word' to the first number of his weekly journal *Household Words* (30 March 1850), in which he announces that one of the journal's aims will be 'to show to all, that in all familiar things ... there is Romance enough, if we will find it out'. Referring to the technological triumphs of the age, he says, 'The swart giants, Slaves of the Lamp of Knowledge, have their thousand and one tales, no less than the Genii of the East; and these, in all their wild, grotesque, and fanciful aspects ... we design to tell.'

For Dickens this perception of romantic elements in steam-engines and industrial processes is intimately connected with what he announces as one of the journal's principal objectives, namely to 'tenderly cherish' in all its readers, young and old, rich and poor

> ... that light of Fancy which is inherent in the human breast; which, according to its nurture, burns with an inspiring flame, or sinks into a sullen glare, but which (or woe betide the day!) can never be extinguished. To ... teach the hardest workers at this whirling wheel of toil, that their lot is not necessarily a moody, brutal fact, excluded from the sympathies and graces of imagination; to bring the greater and the lesser in degree, together, upon that wide field, and mutually dispose them to a better acquaintance and a kinder understanding – is one main object of our Household Words.

Dickens, in fact, profoundly believed not only that the 'fusion of the graces of imagination with the realities of life' was 'vital to the welfare of any community' ('A Last Household Word', *HW*, 28 May 1859) and that 'a nation without fancy, without some romance, never did, never can, never will, hold a great place under the sun' ('Frauds on the Fairies') he also saw works of the imagination – art, in fact – as crucially important to the reconcilement of classes and the development of social harmony. Continued failure to nurture Fancy in the lives of the masses was the 'terrible mistake of these days' which inspired him to write his *Household Words* novel *Hard Times*, with its warnings of the dangers of an English-style French Revolution:

> Utilitarian economists, skeletons of schoolmasters, Commissioners of Fact, genteel and used-up infidels, gabblers of many little dog's-eared creeds, the poor you will have always with you. Cultivate in them, while there is yet

time, the utmost graces of the fancies and affections, to
adorn their lives so much in need of ornament; or, in the
day of your triumph, when romance is utterly driven out
of their soul, and they and a bare existence stand face to
face, Reality will take a wolfish turn, and make an end of
you. (*HT*, II. 6)

This exhortation follows immediately upon Dickens's description of the tender parting in a dreary Coketown street of
two 'hands', the blighted lovers Stephen and Rachel, as the
former, victim of both Capital and Labour in this grimly polit-
ico-economic town, is about to leave in search of work
elsewhere. Dickens firmly links 'fancies', products of the
imagination, with the human capacity for forming loving relationships ('affections') and evokes the spectre of the French
Revolution as a dire warning of what, in his view, will come to
pass in England if the masses are starved of all 'romance' and
brutalised.

At the end of *Hard Times* Dickens gives us a glimpse of
what Louisa's future will be like as, 'with a gentler and humbler
face', she returns to her childhood habit of imagining pictures
of the future in the fire. She has recoiled from the last step of
Mrs Sparsit's staircase but has come so near to being a fallen
woman that, in accordance with the iron laws of Victorian
fiction, there can be for her no happy turning to a new and
fruitful marriage and motherly concern that children of her own
'should have a childhood of the mind no less than a childhood
of the body'. Instead, it seems that she is to become a sort of
universal aunt, 'grown learned in childish lore', who will not
only cultivate every 'innocent and pretty fancy' in the world of
the child but will also try hard

... to know her humbler fellow-creatures, and to beautify
their lives of machinery and reality with those imaginative graces and delights, without which the heart of

infancy will wither up, the sturdiest physical manhood will be morally stark death, and the plainest National Prosperity figures can show, will be the Writing on the Wall ... .

As is clear from his 'Preliminary Word', Dickens saw his mission as 'Conductor' of *Household Words* very much in the light of Louisa's 'beautification' of the lives of the Coketown operatives, even though the journal was inevitably destined for a more middle class than working class readership. It cost two pence a week as opposed to the penny charged for the Chartist G. W. M. Reynolds's highly successful weekly *Reynolds's Miscellany*, begun four years earlier. Reynolds's adroit mixture of sensationalist serials – the first one was entitled 'Wagner the Werewolf' – and political propaganda specifically addressed to 'the industrial classes' was anathema to Dickens. For him men like Reynolds were but a 'draggled fringe on the Red Cap [of Liberty], Panders to the basest passions of the lowest natures'. Both in his own essays and in those of all his contributors Dickens was constantly concerned to 'keep Household Words imaginative!' This was he told Wills his 'solemn and continual Conductorial Injunction' and Wills (whom Dickens once described as 'a capital fellow for his work, but decidedly of the Nutmeg-Grater or Fancy-Bread-Rasper-School') was often the recipient of complaints like the following:

... the No. is an awfully and solemnly heavy one – and ... must really be lightened. I read it last night and had a Nightmare. I doubt if anything so heavy (except stewed lead) could possibly be taken, before going to bed .... The 'Stereoscope' is dreadfully literal. Some fancy must be got into the No .... I should have thought the greater part of it written by McCulloch [the statistician and economist, J. R. McCulloch], edited by Rintoul [editor of *The Spectator*] ... .

And Dickens adds a P.S. 'Brighten it, brighten it, brighten it!'

Dickens was constantly preoccupied with ensuring that the journalism published in his magazine should combine factual truth ('nothing', he once wrote to Wills, 'can be so damaging to us as inaccuracy') with writing that should stimulate and feed the imagination and thereby, as he passionately believed, raise the reader's moral awareness. This flowed naturally from his lofty conception of his art and of the responsibilities attached to his phenomenal popularity.

He had a particular distaste for crudely didactic, moralising fiction, perhaps because it could be seen as a gross caricature of what he himself sought to do. He especially disliked it when it was directed towards children, like the books given out at Charley Hexam's Ragged School, where the offence is compounded by the 'grimly ludicrous pretence' that such works were appropriate reading for the street-children of the slums:

> Young women old in the vices of the commonest and worst life, were expected to profess themselves enthralled by the good child's book, the *Adventures of Little Margery*, who resided in the village cottage by the mill; severely reproved and morally squashed the miller when she was five and he was fifty; divided her porridge with the singing birds; denied herself a new nankeen bonnet, on the grounds that the turnips did not wear nankeen bonnets, neither did the sheep who ate them; who plaited straw and delivered the dreariest orations to all comers, at all sorts of unseasonable times. (*OMF*, II. 1)

Dickens was horrified when his former friend and illustrator George Cruikshank adapted traditional fairy-tales in order to propagandise for teetotalism or vegetarianism or whatever — hence the devastating parody of Cruikshank's 'Cinderella' he included in his *Household Words* article 'Frauds on the Fairies':

Then, she [the Fairy Godmother] sent [Cinderella] for six mice from the mouse-trap, which she changed into prancing horses, free from the obnoxious and oppressive post-horse duty. Then, to the rat-trap in the stable for a rat, which she changed to a state-coachman, not amenable to the iniquitous assessed taxes. Then, to look behind a watering-pot for six lizards, which she changed into six footmen, each with a petition in his hand ready to present to the Prince, signed by fifty thousand persons, in favour of the early closing movement. (*HW*, 1 Oct. 1853)

It is true that in his own *Christmas Carol*, Dickens does smuggle in a passing bit of anti-Malthusian or anti-Sabbatarianism propaganda but the moral of the story as a whole is of much wider application, concerned with inculcating lessons of love, charity, pity, sympathy, and so on (in his review for *Fraser's Magazine* Thackeray pronounced that the little book was 'a national benefit and to every man and woman who reads it a personal kindness'). So, too, with nearly all his writings, fictional or non-fictional. He wrote always with a grand humanitarian purpose. 'Pray do not … suppose', he wrote to one correspondent (20 December 1852):

> … that I ever write merely to amuse, or without an object. I may try to insinuate it into people's hearts sometimes, in preference to knocking them down and breaking their heads with it (which I have observed them apt to resent, and then they fall upon the object and do it an injury) but I always have it. Without it, my pursuit – and the steadiness, patience, seclusion, regularity, hard work, and self-concentration it demands – would be utterly worthless to me. I should die at the oar, and could die a more contemptible and worthless death in no man's eyes than in my own.

Six years later he was writing to his fellow-novelist Catherine Gore,

> I hope I have done my part to make the rising generation "more childish", in rendering them a little more imaginative, a little more gentle, and a little less conceited and hard, than they would have been without me. I desire to do nothing better. (3 Jan. 1859)

Behind all his satirical attacks on particular institutions — workhouses, bad schools, the 'solitary system' in prisons, the Court of Chancery, the Civil Service, etc. — lay this grand and urgent concern with human brotherhood and sisterhood, with mutual kindness, benevolence, justice and freedom. The greatest of all Dickens critics, G.K. Chesterton, hit the nail on the head (as he so often did) when he wrote that Dickens was 'not against any institution so much as against a certain expression on the human face', that expression being one of a denial of shared humanity.

His great weapon for 'insinuating his object into people's hearts' was 'Fancy', the creation of stories, characters, 'fancifully photographic' descriptions in novels and journalistic essays — all aimed at influencing his readers' behaviour and attitudes towards others, especially towards the less fortunate. A letter of Robert Louis Stevenson's quoted in *The Dickensian* (1920) provides us with a dramatic example of Dickens's desired effect in operation:

> I wonder if you have ever read Dickens's Christmas Books? ... they are too much perhaps. I have read only two yet, but I have cried my eyes out, and had a terrible fight not to sob. But oh, dear God, they are good — and I feel so good after them — I shall do good and lose no time — I want to go out and comfort someone — I shall give money. Oh, what a jolly thing it is for a man to have

written books like these and just filled people's hearts with pity.

And allusion to it featured prominently in Dean Stanley's obituary sermon in Westminster Abbey:

He whose loss we now mourn occupied a greater space than any other writer in the minds of Englishmen during the last thirty-three years. We read him, talked about him, acted him; we laughed with him; we were roused by him to a consciousness of the misery of others, and to a pathetic interest in human life. Works of fiction, indirectly, are great instructors of this world …

Dickens saw his art as something held 'in trust' from God for the benefit of humanity and he had the same exalted idea regarding the work of his fellow-artists in other fields such as his beloved and revered friend, the 'eminent tragedian' W. C. Macready, or his equally beloved painter friend Daniel Maclise. Having studied Maclise's cartoon for his 'Spirit of Chivalry' fresco in the House of Lords, for example, Dickens wrote an article praising it to the skies for its inspirational qualities, for being 'a composition of such marvellous beauty … of such vigorous and skilful drawing, of such thought and *fancy* [my italics], … subserving one grand harmony and one plain purpose … ' (A far cry, evidently, from those degraded and degrading paintings hanging in Mr Carker's home in *Dombey and Son*, 33, that 'do not commemorate great thoughts or deeds, or render nature in the poetry of landscape, hall, or hut, but are of one voluptuous cast – mere shows of form and colour').

*

It is not surprising that two of the most convincingly evil characters in all Dickens's books should be Skimpole, in *Bleak House*, and another of Fancy's Traitors, the cynical and dilettante painter Henry Gowan in *Little Dorrit* who is described by Daniel Doyce (Dickens's portrait of a true artist, even though he is supposed to be an inventor) as having 'sauntered into the Arts at a leisurely Pall-Mall pace'. The self-tormenting Miss Wade's imagination is corrupted by paranoia but it can still enable her to register the sinister nature of this man in a vivid 'fancy':

> He was like the dressed-up Death in the Dutch series; whatever figure he took upon his arm, whether it was youth or age, beauty or ugliness, whether he danced with it, sang with it, played with it, or prayed with it, he made it ghastly. (*LD*, II. 21)

Here is Gowan telling Arthur Clennam of his fear that his disappointment at not having obtained a government sinecure despite all his family connections, may damage his ability to keep up the hypocritical game that, he asserts, he and his fellow-artists are all playing:

> 'To help myself in my turn, as the man before me helped himself in his, and pass the bottle of smoke. To keep up the pretence as to labour, and study, and patience, and being devoted to my art … and all the rest of it – in short, to pass the bottle of smoke, according to rule.'

> 'But it is well for a man to respect his own vocation, whatever it is; and to think himself bound to uphold it, and to claim for it the respect it deserves; is it not?' Arthur reasoned. 'And your vocation, Gowan, may really demand this suit and service. I confess that I should have thought all Art did.' (*LD*, I. 34)

Clennam's response provokes merely derision as Gowan laughs at him for living in 'such a rose-coloured mist'.

We may link this portrait of an artist betraying his art directly with the mid-Victorian 'Dignity of Literature' debate in which Dickens found himself ranged against Thackeray. There seems to be absolutely no grounds for the assertion sometimes made that Dickens based the character of Gowan on Thackeray, but we may note that he did feel constrained in his obituary of his 'old comrade and brother-in-arms' to comment that he felt Thackeray had 'too much feigned a want of earnestness, and ... made a pretence of undervaluing his art, which was not good for the art he held in trust'. Dickens had much disapproved of Thackeray's *Punch* parodies of Edward Bulwer, Disraeli and other novelists, telling Forster that he believed 'they did no honor to literature or to literary men, and should be left to very miserable and inferior hands' (9 June 1847) and had later remonstrated with Thackeray himself: 'I think it is a great pity to take advantage of the means our calling gives us with such accursed readiness, of at all depreciating or vulgarising each other' (we notice that literature is for Dickens a 'calling' rather than a trade or a profession).

This concern, deriving from his high conception of the artist's mission as the champion of Fancy, was closely linked with his political attitudes as we can see from what he said in a speech to the Newsvendors' Benevolent Institution (27 Jan. 1852) when he praised Forster (who had recently published a biography of Goldsmith detailing the terrible struggles the author of Dickens's beloved *Vicar of Wakefield* had had to keep afloat) as

... the gallant champion of the dignity of literature and its common cause with the people against sordid patrons, hard taskmasters, empty headed noodles, and every description of froth and foppery that could possibly surround them.

He returned to the theme in another speech the following year at a banquet in his honour in Birmingham:

> From the shame of the purchased dedication ... from that venality which, by a fine moral retribution, has degraded statesmen even to a greater extent than authors, because the statesman entertained a low belief in the universality of corruption, while the author yielded only to the dire necessity of his calling, – from all such evils the people have set Literature free.

And many years later, at another banquet in his honour (in Liverpool, 1869) he said that when he had first taken literature as his profession it had seemed to him 'that it was not so well understood in England as it was in other countries that literature was a dignified profession, by which any man might stand or fall'. Twenty-one years before he had written to Thackeray, in the letter already quoted which was replying to his brother-novelist's eulogy of *Dombey and Son*:

> I do sometimes please myself with thinking that my success has opened the way for good writers. And of this, I am now quite sure, and hope I shall be when I die – that in all my social doings, I am mindful of this honour and dignity and always try to do something towards the quiet assertion of their right place. I am always possessed with the hope of leaving the position of literary men in England, something better and more independent than I found it. (9 Jan. 1848)

No one in his day was a more energetic champion of artists and writers than Dickens. He fought long and hard, though in the end unsuccessfully, to reform and make more effective the Royal Literary Fund, established to dispense charity to impoverished writers. He also worked hard, though again without ultimate success, with his friend and fellow-novelist Bulwer to set up a so-called 'Guild of Literature and Art' to provide housing and financial help for writers and artists fallen on hard times. Given the overwhelming importance, both for the individual and for the nation, that Dickens, as documented in this chapter, attached to 'Fancy' or the life of the imagination, his somewhat strenuous insistence on the Dignity of Literature and his generous expenditure of time and energy in attempts to benefit writers and artists becomes entirely understandable.

Innocence

It is good to be children, sometimes, and never better than at Christmas, when its mighty Founder was a child himself.

A Christmas Carol

When I go into the City, now, it makes me sorrowful to think that I am quite an artful wretch. Strolling about it as a lost child, I thought of a British Merchant and the Lord Mayor, and was full of reverence. Strolling about it now, I laugh at the sacred liveries of state, and get indignant with the corporation as one of the strongest practical jokes of the present day.

'Gone Astray', *HW*, 13 Aug. 1853

All my early readings and early imaginations dated from this place, and I took them away so full of innocent construction and guileless belief, and I brought them back so worn and torn, so much the wiser and so much the worse!

UT, 'Dullborough Town' (*ATYR*, 30 June 1860)

I once knew a history teacher who gave his students the following sentence as a sort of mantra to help guide them through the complexities of 16th-century European history: 'It was a pity — there had to be a Reformation'. This acknowledged the terrible wars and devastation that resulted from the great upheaval but recognised also that it had been necessary and even desirable.

We might adapt the formula to express Dickens on childhood as follows: 'It is a pity – we have to grow up'. This does not mean, however, that he would have been charmed by the idea of Barrie's *Peter Pan*. Adult Dickens characters who ask to be treated as though they were still children are either objects of pathos (if female) or, as regards the single male example, both contemptible and treacherous. David Copperfield's 'child-wife' Dora, trapped by her upbringing as a sort of pet or pretty toy, is no Ibsenite Nora. She is quite unable to precipitate herself into responsible adulthood and, with symbolic appropriateness, dies in childbirth. *David Copperfield* is as a novel centrally concerned with the dangers of too much innocence and with the necessity of growing up into responsible maturity. David, whose innocent trust in Steerforth loses Mr Mell his job and leads to the desolation of the Peggotty home, must leave behind his 'Davy', 'Daisy' and 'Doady' selves and become 'Trotwood Copperfield', what Aunt Betsey calls 'a fine, firm fellow with a will of [his] own'. In such a book poor Dora cannot survive except (crucially for David's mental and spiritual health) as an unfading memory for him of fairy-like charm and beauty.

The mentally retarded Maggie in *Little Dorrit* is, of course, deeply pathetic in a different way, a grotesque-looking grown woman of 'about eight-and-twenty' who, as Little Dorrit tells Clennam, 'had a bad fever' when she was ten years old, after years of physical abuse at the hands of a drunken grandmother, and 'has never grown any older ever since' (*LD*, I, 9). She clings to Little Dorrit as her 'Little Mother' and remembers her time in a beneficent hospital with the happiness of a child ('Such lemonades! Such oranges! Such Chicking! Oh, AIN'T it a delightful place to go and stop at!'). Quite another matter is Skimpole in *Bleak House* who calls himself 'a mere child in the world'. What he is, in fact, is an artful parasite battening on 'jaundiced' John Jarndyce's desperate need to find childlike innocence somewhere in his 'crafty' world of Chancery suits and 'wiglomeration'. Jarndyce delights in Skimpole because he believes of him that 'in simplicity, and freshness, and enthusiasm, and a fine guileless inaptitude for all worldly affairs, he is a perfect child'. And when Esther offers him a way of avoiding coming to the obvious conclusion after Skimpole has cunningly extracted money to pay his debts from the true innocents Richard and Ada, he jumps at it:

> I ventured to take this opportunity of hinting that Mr Skimpole, being in all such matters quite a child –
> 'Eh, my dear?' said Mr Jarndyce, catching at the word.
> '– Being quite a child, sir,' said I, 'and so different from other people –'
> 'You are right!' said Mr Jarndyce, brightening. 'Your woman's wit hits the mark. He is a child – an absolute child. I told you he was a child, you know, when I first mentioned him.' (*BH*, 6)

The power with which Dickens portrays Skimpole in his full odiousness (perhaps the most purely evil act in the book is his betrayal, for a monetary bribe, of the whereabouts of the pathetic fugitive Jo) surely derives from the fact that this figure parodies a type of character the conception of which evidently gave great delight to Dickens's imagination, the male 'grown-up child'. This character, adult in years but as guileless as children were supposed to be, is always trusting, simple-hearted and quickly moved to sympathy for anyone in trouble or distress. Between the glorious prototype, Mr Pickwick (whose heart, says Sam Weller, 'must ha' been born five-and-twenty year arter his body, at least') and Twemlow, that 'innocent piece of dinner-furniture' in *Our Mutual Friend*, Dickens presents his readers with the type in many different, but always male, forms. To name some of the most notable, we have the Cheeryble Brothers in *Nickleby* (whom Orwell famously castigated as 'a pair of gruesome old Peter Pans'), Mr

Toots in *Dombey*, Tom Pinch in *Chuzzlewit*, Mr Dick and Dr. Strong in *Copperfield*, and Joe Gargery in *Great Expectations*, whom the young Pip 'always treated ... as a larger species of child, and as no more than [his] equal'. We might add to these characters a whole group from *Hard Times*, the circus folk (men *and* women in this case) in Mr Sleary's troupe about whom, Dickens writes, 'there was a remarkable gentleness and childishness ... a special inaptitude for any kind of sharp practice, and an untiring readiness to help and pity one another' (*HT*, I.6)

It is no accident that these providers of popular entertainment should figure in the catalogue of Dickensian innocents since a capacity for child-like delight in all forms of theatre goes along with that keen enjoyment of stories of wonder and adventure that is so prominent a characteristic of the type. Tom Pinch is transported by the bookshop windows in Salisbury

> ... where poor Robinson Crusoe stood alone in his might, with dog and hatchet, goat-skin-cap and fowling-pieces; calmly surveying Philip Quarll and the host of imitators round him, and calling Mr Pinch to witness that he, of all the crowd, impressed one solitary footprint on the shore of boyish memory, whereof the tread of generations should not stir the lightest grain of sand. (MC, ch. 5)

It is his ability to have such vivid recall of specific boyhood memories and emotions that distinguishes Tom Pinch as the typical Dickensian grown-up innocent. And it was while writing this novel, *Martin Chuzzlewit*, that Dickens created Tom's polar opposite, old Ebenezer Scrooge, the man who has virtually dehumanised himself by the rigid suppression of all such memories and the first stage of whose redemption consists in his being made literally to revisit and re-experience his distant past. Nine years later, Dickens wrote for the New Year's Day

1853 number of *Household Words* a remarkable essay entitled
'Where We Stopped Growing'. It begins:

> Few people who have been much in the society of chil-
> dren, are likely to be ignorant of the sorrowful feeling
> sometimes awakened in the mind by the idea of a favour-
> ite child's 'growing up'. This is intelligible enough.
> Childhood is usually so beautiful and engaging, that ...
> there is a mournful shadow of the common lot in the
> notion of its changing and fading into anything else. The
> sentiment is unreasoning and vague, and does not shape
> itself into a wish. To consider what the dependent little
> creature would do without us, or in the course of how few
> years it would be in as bad a condition as those terrible
> immortals upon earth, engendered in the gloom of
> SWIFT'S wise fancy [i. e., the 'Struldbrugs' in *Gulliver's
> Travels*, Part 3] is not within the range of so fleeting a
> thought.

Clearly, there is no yearning for Peter-Panhood here. But
Dickens goes on to consider how childhood may survive bene-
ficently in the adult through the vivid memory of particular
stories, scenes, people or things that made so big an impact on
the child's imagination that no amount of subsequent mundane
experience of the same subject has been able to efface it. And
he begins, interestingly enough, with Tom Pinch's hero, Robinson Crusoe:

> We have never grown the thousandth part of an inch out
> of Robinson Crusoe. He fits us just as well, and in exactly
> the same way, as when we were among the smallest of
> the small ... .

There follows a long paragraph of apparently effortless
recall of dozens of details from the novel comparable to his

remembering marvel after marvel from *The Arabian Nights* in 'A Christmas Tree' (see above, p. 25). The list in 'Where We Stopped Growing' continues with other books, objects, places and people that still affect Dickens just as they had done when first encountered in his childhood (including two demented old women wandering the London streets, one of them 'dressed entirely in white'). So long as such memories remain available to us, instantly retrievable in all their vivid particularity, we shall never, Dickens believes, altogether lose that innocence we had when we were children, 'fresh from the hands of God' (*MHC*), nor all the qualities that he sees as trooping with such innocence – delighted belief in imaginary worlds, spontaneity, aptness for giving and receiving pleasure through play, readiness to feel sorry for anyone who is unhappy or suffering.

The time of year that would seem most obviously propitious for this re-emergence of the child surviving within us is 'Happy, happy Christmas, that can win us back to the delusions of our childish days!' (*PP*, 28), the great annual festival when people naturally recall the past, and when, Dickens writes,

> … we all come home, or ought to come home, for a short holiday – the longer, the better from the great boarding-school, where we are for ever working at our arithmetical slates, to take, and give a rest. (*CS*, 'A Christmas Tree'.)

It is a time for parties, games, dances – pleasures to bring out the child in us, and in which the Dickensian grown-up innocent naturally takes enormous delight. Mr Pickwick, for example, is a leading light in all the Christmas revels at Dingley Dell, including taking his turn upon the ice (asked if he slides, he replies, 'I used to do so, on the gutters when I was a boy') and the fast-becoming-converted Scrooge is transported by the games he sees being played at his nephew's party; like a child, he begs the Ghost of Christmas Present to let him stay there longer (' "Here's a new game,' said Scrooge, "One half hour, Spirit, only one!" ').

It is hardly surprising, therefore, that Christmas, and what Dickens called his 'Carol philosophy', should have been so central to his whole oeuvre, and indeed such an important occasion in his own domestic life. For him it was the great Festival of Innocence when the one being in all recorded history who remained all his life perfectly good and innocent, a sort of sublime version of the grown-up child, was in literal fact a child (we shall be looking at Dickens's personal brand of Christianity in a later chapter). In her book, *My Father As I Recall Him* (1897), his elder daughter Mamie devotes her second chapter to glowing reminiscences of family Christmas and New Year celebrations:

> Christmas was always a time which in our home was looked forward to with eagerness and delight, and to my father it was a time dearer than any other part of the year, I think. He loved Christmas for its deep significance as well as for its joys ....

> [He] always deserted work for the week, and that was almost our greatest treat. He was the fun and life of those gatherings, the true Christmas spirit of sweetness and hospitality. Long walks with him were daily treats to be remembered. Games passed our evening merrily.

From 1843 onwards Dickens also became Christmas storyteller to the nation at large, a role that he continues posthumously to fulfil, although the story now is always the same one and the *Carol*'s successor Christmas Books and all the Christmas stories contributed to his weekly magazines over a period of seventeen years are pretty much forgotten.

It is noticeable, in the passage quoted above from 'A Christ-

mas Tree', that Dickens, seeking an image to express the survival of the child within the adult, chooses one that is both
distinctively middle-class and entirely male in its implications
(in her book Mamie refers to 'the boys', i. e., her numerous
brothers, coming 'home for the holidays' and being at once
plunged into rehearsals for Christmas and New Year domestic
entertainments). Both in the world of Dickens's imagination
and in the real-life middle-class world he inhabited, women
were not away from home 'working at arithmetical slates' in the
great boarding-school of the public world. They would either
be young girls still under the parental roof, presumed to be full
of innocently 'romantic' ideas about future husbands, or else
they would be wives and mothers in their own homes, closely
associated with children and 'protected' from worldly cares.

For Dickens female innocence is not solely a matter of class
or economic status, however. Again and again in his writings,
both public and private, he testifies to the belief that he shared
with so many of his contemporaries (called 'detestable cant' by
John Stuart Mill, author of *The Subjection of Women*) that
women's nature is essentially higher than men's and 'ever, in
the mass, better, truer, higher, nobler, quicker to feel, and much
more constant to retain, all tenderness and pity, self-denial and
devotion' (*DS*, 3); and that, as he wrote to the philanthropist
Miss Coutts à propos her support for Ragged Schools, 'there is
much more Good in Women than in Men, however Ragged
they are' (24 Sept. 1843). Inevitably, however, his artist's
imagination tends to be more stirred by Magdalens than by
Madonnas and his first major female character, the prostitute
Nancy in *Oliver Twist*, protector of the child-hero's sturdy
innocence, remains one of his most memorable creations –
though few, I imagine, would now agree with Wilkie Collins
that it was 'the finest thing he ever did'. She is also the first of
a long line of Dickens female characters from very different
class backgrounds who have 'fallen' from innocence. The fall
may be presented by him as the result of many different things

and it takes many forms – seduction (Rosa Dartle and Little Em'ly in *Copperfield*), the desperation of extreme poverty (Lilian in *The Chimes*), mercenary or manipulative mothers or mother-substitutes (Edith Dombey, Estella in *Great Expectations*). Almost always there is, sooner or later, on the fallen one's part, as in the case of Nancy, a painful awareness of loss and debasement leading to penitence and/or desire for atonement (Rosa Dartle is an interesting exception here). Of course, in real life Dickens certainly met many women who did not at all conform to this pattern – such, for example, as that 'most deceitful little minx' Sesina, a very temporary resident at Miss Coutts's Home for Homeless Women, whom he had to send away pretty quickly (she would, he said, 'corrupt a Nunnery in a fortnight') – but this does not seem to have at all affected his essentialist belief in the innate moral and spiritual superiority of women.

We can now perhaps see why there are no female characters in the list of Dickens's 'grown-up innocents' given above. It is not until he comes to write *Little Dorrit* (his most profound novel apart from *Our Mutual Friend*) that he engages with the idea of an unmarried female grown-up child. Amy Dorrit, is the Child of the Marshalsea Prison in which she was born, but at the opening of the story she is a woman in years and, having been immersed from her birth in a world of shamed poverty, she has inevitably learned all about the needy miseries and desperate survival strategies belonging to such a world yet somehow has retained an essential unworldly innocence of which her diminutive child-like stature is the outward and visible sign. In her loving devotion to her long-imprisoned widowed father, her shiftless brother and her volatile sister, she has contrived to exploit every possible opportunity offered by the world of the debtors' prison to better their lives. She has become 'worldly wise in hard and poor necessities' but remains 'innocent in all things else', especially with regard to the moral degeneracy of her sponging old father whom she continues to see through 'a mist', like the way she sees the prison itself and 'the turbid living river that flowed through it and flowed on' (*LD*, I.7). Even at his most debased in the reader's (and his own) eyes she is still able, Dickens writes, to comfort his 'wasted heart' by taking it upon

> ... her innocent breast, and turning to it a fountain of love and fidelity that never ran dry or waned through all his years of famine. (1. 19)

This somewhat startling image, deriving from Classical legend, is uncharacteristically baroque for Dickens. With its strong sexual overtones, mingling the maternal and the erotic, barely controlled by the adjective 'innocent', it signals, I believe, the strain that he feels in his efforts to present at full length a character who is a grown-up woman with a woman's body, however diminutive, but at the same time child-like in her purity and trustfulness.

For it is sexuality and sexual awareness that seems to be the ultimate dividing-line between innocence and non-innocence in Dickens and this is the one aspect of childhood innocence that cannot be revisited or revived within the adult – even in Christmas games – hence the strange combination of wistfulness, voyeurism and something approaching rape-fantasy in the following passage of authorial commentary in *A Christmas Carol* which describes 'a beautiful young girl', the daughter of Scrooge's former fiancée, joining in some rough-and-tumble games with her younger siblings:

> [she] got pillaged by the young brigands most ruthlessly. What would I not have given to be one of them! Though I never would have been so rude, no, no! I wouldn't for the wealth of all the world have crushed that braided hair, and torn it down ... . As to measuring her waist in sport, as they did, bold young brood, I couldn't have done it; I

should have expected my arm to have grown round it for a punishment, and never come straight again. And yet I should have dearly liked, I own, to have touched her lips; to have looked upon the lashes of her downcast eyes, and never raised a blush; to have let loose waves of hair, an inch of which would be a keepsake beyond price: in short, I should have liked, I do confess, to have had the lightest license of a child, and yet to have been man enough to know its value.

'To have the lightest license of a child, and yet to have been man enough to know its value': what can this high-sounding phrase mean but 'to have unrestrained, non-sexual, physical contact with the girl in the way children are free to have but at the same time to enjoy, unreproved, the adult pleasure of sexual stimulation that such contact would give me'? The impossibility of such a wish is made clear in a very different sort of passage in a very different story when the unnamed prostitute whom Little Dorrit encounters in the midnight streets of London at first mistakes her for a child and Maggie for her irresponsible mother:

'Kiss a poor lost creature, dear,' she said, bending her face, 'and tell me where she's taking you.'
Little Dorrit turned towards her.
'Why, my God!' she said, recoiling, 'you're a woman!'

Full of concern, Little Dorrit says, 'Let me speak to you as if I really were a child' but is repulsed: the woman says, 'You can't do it … . You are kind and innocent; but you can't look at me out of a child's eyes' (*LD*, I.14). Little Dorrit, that is to say, must inevitably be aware that the woman trades, however remorsefully, in sex and there is no way, therefore, that she can look at her in the way that that icon of innocence Oliver Twist, say, could look at Nancy.

The bleak finality of this exchange notwithstanding, there are several places in Dickens's novels and stories where he indulges his fantasy of 'innocent sex' by portraying in wholly 'innocent' terms a relationship that would normally carry sexual connotations – for example, the quasi-marital household of those 'two little sparklers' as he fondly called them in a letter, the grown-up innocent Tom Pinch and his equally innocent sister Ruth (*MC*, ch. 39). Examples of childhood sweethearts ('innocent' by definition, as it were) occur often in his writings, the most famous being that of the young David and Little Em'ly in the early part of *Copperfield*. In his 'written memory' the older David looks fondly back to the time when he and Em'ly exchanged 'an innocent kiss under the lee of [Mr Peggotty's] lobster-outhouse' and records:

> I am sure I loved that baby quite as truly, quite as tenderly, with greater purity and more disinterestedness, than can enter into the best love of a later time of life, high and ennobling as it is. I am sure my fancy raised up something around that blue-eyed mite of a child, which etherealised and made a very angel of her .... (*DC*, 3)

The most insistent childhood-sweetheart example appears in 'The Holly-tree Inn', a multiple-authored story that formed the *Household Words* Christmas number for 1855. Among the sections written by Dickens himself was the chapter entitled 'The Boots'. This concerns two small children eloping together who arrive at the Holly Tree en route for Gretna Green and are recognised by Cobbs 'the Boots', an intensely sympathetic inn-servant who had previously worked for the little boy's father. Cobbs dwells on the charm of seeing the children acting like a courting couple and on the poignancy of his feelings while he was arranging for them to be restored to their families:

> ... he wished with all his heart there was any impossible
> place where those two babies could make an impossible
> marriage, and live impossibly happy ever afterwards.

Another aspect of Dickens's fascination with the idea of 'innocent' sexuality is closely linked with his passion for the stories referred to in the previous chapter, those that fed his childhood imagination. Many of these were decidedly 'adult' in their presentation of male/female relations but were then read by him purely for their exotic, romantic or adventurous appeal. In the description of how the imaginative life of the young David Copperfield was sustained in the darkest period of his childhood by reading the novels of Smollett, Fielding, Cervantes and others, as well as The *Arabian Nights*, (a passage that Forster tells us was literally autobiographical on Dickens's part), the older David comments, [these stories] 'did me no harm; for, whatever harm was in some of them, was not there for me; I knew nothing of it. ' He played at being Tom Jones but it was 'a child's Tom Jones, a harmless creature'. No infantile Molly Seagrim featured in his play, we should understand. The autobiographical element is much more concealed and oblique in 'The Haunted House', the first Christmas story for *All The Year Round* (1859). In this Dickens writes as a man who finds himself haunted by 'the Ghost in Master B's Room', the ghost, that is, of the child that he had once been. Scrooge is shown his former self as a child by the Ghost of Christmas Past but the narrator in 'The Haunted House' actually becomes his child self again and re-lives an episode from that time. At school with one other little boy and eight little girls, he is inspired by reading *The Arabian Nights* to organise himself and the others as Caliph, Grand Vizier and a Seraglio without any of them 'entertaining the faintest doubts of the meritorious character of the Oriental establishment [they] proposed to import'. The sudden news of his father's death, his return home to find there 'Debt ... as well as Death', and his being sent 'to a great, cold, bare, school of big boys … where everybody, large and small, was cruel' puts an abrupt end to innocence and the story ends with a lament for its passing:

> Ah me, ah me! No other ghost has haunted the boy's room, my friends, since I have occupied it than the ghost of my own childhood, the ghost of my own innocence, the ghost of my own airy belief ….

Nevertheless, he continues his life and work as an adult, he says, 'as cheerfully and thankfully as I may'. It was a pity – he had to grow up.

Dickens's obviously intense need to believe in the innocence of 'unfallen' women leads him to negotiate the problem that his ideal young wives must inevitably know about sex by presenting them, from Mrs Chirrup in *Sketches of Young Couples* (1840) onwards, in child-like terms as far as possible, but also as having a special aptitude for domestic science and household management. They must at least have, like Bella Wilfer and unlike poor Dora, a willingness and an ability to learn these things, as seen in Bella's struggles with that 'sage volume', *The Complete British Family Housewife*:

> … which she would sit consulting, with her elbows on the table and her temples on her hands, like some perplexed enchantress poring over the Black Art … . And … with all her dimples screwed into an expression of profound research … (*OMF*, IV. 5)

And, of course, Bella, whom her husband addresses as 'My dear child', can only refer to her pregnancy by means of bashful metaphor: 'I think … there is a ship upon the ocean … bringing … to you and me … a little baby, John.'

By the same token, he is strongly drawn to presenting little girls behaving like innocent little mothers or little companion-

able wives (the two roles seem to melt into one) to their fathers
– or, in Little Nell's case, to their grandfathers. This is the role
that the young Florence Dombey so yearns to play; she watches
with pain a neighbouring child caring for her widowed father:

> The elder child remained with her father when the rest
> had gone away, and made his tea for him – happy little
> housekeeper that she was then! – and sat conversing with
> him … . He made her his companion, though she was
> some years younger than Florence; and she could be as
> staid and pleasantly demure, with her little book or work-
> box, as a woman. (*DS*, 18)

Florence has to wait until she has grown up and become an
actual mother, and until after Dombey's pride has been hum-
bled to the dust, before she can take on the role, her assumption
of which is marked by a tableau that anticipates *Little Dorrit*'s
Roman-daughter one ('Upon the breast that he had bruised,
against the heart that he had almost broken, she laid his face …').
But in the next novel, *Copperfield*, Dickens elaborates the
anonymous child-figure observed by Florence into Agnes
Wickfield, the novel's 'true heroine' and from very early on in
her life her widowed father's beloved 'little housekeeper'. In
the following chapter we shall see that there is, with regard to
society at large, a darker side to this reversal of the parent-child
relationship that is so markedly recurrent a situation in Dickens's
fiction but here I am only concerned to note its usefulness,
comparable to that of the childhood-sweethearts situation, in
enabling Dickens to portray the role of wife or mother performed 'innocently'.

There is, it is true, in his last completed full-length novel a
remarkably and painfully grotesque version of a young girl
having to take on the role of mother to her own father. The little
crippled dolls' dressmaker, Fanny Cleaver, who gives herself
the more innocent-sounding name of Jenny Wren, has to cope

with a hopelessly alcoholic father and his incorrigible habit of spending on drink the money so desperately needed to keep the struggling little household afloat. She scolds him bitterly like 'a little quaint shrew' while he, an 'indecorous threadbare ruin, from the broken shoes to the prematurely-grey scanty hair', grovels in shame before her. But just before this scene Dickens has been at pains to show that Jenny has not, in spite of her terrible situation in life, been wholly prematurely deprived of her child-nature and its 'innocent' imaginings – she can still smell the flowers and hear the birds that she smelled and heard in the visions of an earlier period of her childhood – 'visions' rather than the 'pleasant fancies' Lizzie Hexam calls them, for Dickens here seeks to elevate the workings of the childish imagination to something approaching the sublime as Jenny describes 'the long bright slanting rows' of children 'all in white dresses, and with something shining ... on their heads' that would come down to her, calling out 'Who is this in pain?', to give her 'delicious ease and rest' (*OMF*, II. 2).

Jenny's childhood innocence has been almost obliterated by the harshness of her struggle for existence. Social deprivation is seen by Dickens as one of the three great enemies of innocence – the forces, that is, that interpose to prevent the 'natural', gradual human development from innocence to experience but act on a child's moral nature rather like the favoured educational system of Mrs Pipchin in *Dombey* which was 'not to encourage a child's mind to develop and expand itself like a young flower, but to open it by force like an oyster'. There are the reprovers and repressers, like Mr Gradgrind and Mr M'Choakumchild and Mr Barlow (*UT*), or like the Murdstones, Miss Barbary (*BH*) and Mrs Clennam (*LD*) who, whether motivated by some grim educational theory or by Calvinist-type religious beliefs, seek to 'kill the robber Fancy' lurking inside the children they have in their power, or to instil in them a sense of shame and guilt. Then there are the exploiters who practise both on children and on grown-up innocents. They are a very motley crew – prominent among them Fagin, Quilp, Pecksniff, Steerforth, Skimpole, Vholes, Silas Wegg – but they all seek to exploit and betray trusting innocents for their own sordid ends. Lastly, there are, as already noted, the horrific social conditions in which such vast numbers of the children of the poor are forced to live, conditions that brutalise them when they are still very young and have to fight for mere physical survival. Such are the children Scrooge is shown by the Ghost of Christmas Present, 'yellow, meagre, ragged, scowling, wolfish', and the ferocious little street-urchin with whom the learned but spiritually desolate Redlaw is juxtaposed in *The Haunted Man*:

> … A face rounded and smoothed by some half-dozen years, but pinched and twisted by the experiences of a life. Bright eyes, but not youthful … . A baby savage, a young monster, a child who had never been a child, a creature who might live to take the outward form of man, but who, within, would live and perish a mere beast.
>
> Used, already, to be worried and hunted like a beast, the boy crouched down as he was looked at, and looked back again, and interposed his arm to ward off the expected blow.
>
> 'I'll bite, ' he said, 'if you hit me!'

In Dickens's earliest writings, the newspaper and periodical sketches and stories collected in *Sketches by Boz*, there are one or two glimpses of childhood innocence in the process of being destroyed by bitter experience of harsh poverty and its exigencies, e. g., the younger of the two girls in 'The Prisoners' Van' who, presumably, have been arrested for prostitution:

> That they were sisters was evident from the resemblance which still subsisted between them, though two additional years of depravity had fixed their brand upon the

elder girl's features, as legibly as if a red-hot iron had seared them. They were both gaudily dressed, the younger one especially … [but] it is impossible to conceive a greater contrast than the demeanour of the two presented. The younger girl was weeping bitterly – not for display, or in the hope of producing effect, but for very shame; her face was buried in her handkerchief: and her whole manner was but too expressive of bitter and unavailing sorrow.

But on the whole Boz's sketches and stories deal more in social satire and local colour than with such themes as innocence and its enemies. It is with the early novels that it becomes such a central concern. *Pickwick Papers* has, indeed, been famously interpreted by W. H. Auden as Dickens's version of the Fall of Man with Mr Pickwick being brought to a knowledge of good and evil through the tutelage of the streetwise but wholly beneficent Sam Weller, the machinations of Dodson and Fogg, and his own eye-opening experiences in the Fleet Prison. Pickwick is a special case, however, a grown-up innocent who, like Tom Pinch later, has a belated but not too painful transition from innocence to a degree at least of awareness of evil. Apart from him Dickens's major icons of innocence are, naturally enough, all children. Oliver Twist, Smike and Little Nell are all threatened (and in Smike's case severely wounded) by various hostile forces, whether social, as represented by Bumble or Squeers or Miss Monflathers (who would send Nell to work in a factory), or else predatory and exploitative like Fagin, Squeers again and Quilp. Essential innocence is preserved in every case though the children have terrifying experiences to endure when they are made vividly aware of the power of evil, whether it be manifested in the social horrors of the workhouse or the Yorkshire school or the nocturnal riots in the 'blackened town' through which Nell and her grandfather have to pass, or in individuals – even loved individuals like

Nell's grandfather when he comes creeping into her room at night to rob her. They preserve themselves by flight and each eventually finds a haven of peace and security presided over by benevolent old bachelors (a haven that in Nell's case is soon exchanged for the more abiding one of heaven itself). In these havens Innocence at last triumphs being unequivocally recognised by all in the approved mode of melodrama. No longer can Oliver be thought a hardened young thief, or Smike simply an idiot, or Nell 'a very wicked little child' because of her association with Jarley's waxworks.

It is fascinating to turn from these early, highly fabular, novels to the last fictional work that Dickens ever completed, a short story written in the first person for an American journal and called 'George Silverman's Explanation' (1868). The profound autobiographical resonances of this remarkable downbeat story have been explored by Dickens scholars, most notably by Harry Stone, but it is as one of Dickens's last and most complex engagements with the concept of innocence that I want to touch on it here. Dickens presents Silverman as a true innocent whose 'Explanation', which he has the utmost difficulty in beginning to write, is a last desperate attempt to achieve an impossible sort of self-recognition, a self-recognition that might possibly lead to public recognition of his own goodness. His 'Explanation' is written in solitude, retirement and distress of mind (in this case he himself is the kindly old bachelor figure in the haven in which he comes to rest but the haven seems to be empty except for graves and he must help himself if he can): he writes out his story, he says, 'for the relief of my own mind, not foreseeing whether or no it will ever have a reader'. We learn that even in his earliest days, in a slum cellar in Preston, he was constantly accused, by his own mother, of being 'a wordly little devil', the very opposite of the innocent that he really is, simply because of his natural child's reactions to elemental things:

Whether I cried for that I was in the dark, or for that it was cold, or for that I was hungry, or whether I squeezed myself into a warm corner where there was a fire, or ate voraciously when there was food, she would still say: 'Oh you worldly little devil!'

As he grows up he seeks obsessively to defend himself against the charge of worldliness by repeated self-sacrifice and self-denial, even to the extent of submitting to what in one part of his mind (he is highly intelligent and wins a scholarship to Cambridge) he knows to be gross exploitation, first by his criminal guardian, Brother Hawkyard and second by his grasping and hypocritical patron Lady Fareway; he likewise suppresses the love he feels, and that he knows would be returned, for Lady Fareway's kind and beautiful daughter. But all his efforts merely lead to more condemnation of him as sullenly selfish or calculatingly worldly as well as bitter accusations from Lady Fareway that he was feathering his own nest. He is almost heart-broken and writes it was only 'little by little' that 'the belief widened that I was not capable of what had been laid to my charge' and he was eventually able to find his haven (which sounds a bit like a pared-down version of Little Nell's remote country church). The feeling at the end of the story is very much one of suffering and of irretrievable loss and exile, of innocence, helpless in the face of its enemies, finding itself identified with its very opposite, tormented and finally driven out of the world. A far cry indeed from the triumphs of Oliver and Nell.

Responsibility and Earnestness

My meaning simply is, that whatever I have tried to do in life, I have tried to do well: that whatever I have devoted myself to, I have devoted myself to completely: that in great aims and in small, I have always been thoroughly in earnest. I have never believed it possible that any natural or improved ability can claim immunity from the companionship of the steady, plain, hard-working qualities, and hope to gain its end …. . Some happy talent, and some fortunate opportunity, may form the two sides of the ladder on which some men mount, but the rounds of that ladder must be made of stuff to stand wear and tear; and there is no substitute for thorough-going, ardent, and sincere earnestness.

David Copperfield, 42

'You do not render justice to your many high powers by thinking too slightingly of what you have in hand, instead of doing it, for the time being, as if there were nothing else to be done in the world — the only likely way I know of, of doing anything. '

Dickens to Henry Morley (contributor to *Household Words*), 31 Oct. 1852

If one had to find a single adjective to express the leading quality that all Dickens's heroes and heroines have in common, from Nicholas Nickleby onwards, a good one to choose would be 'responsible'. The usual pattern is for characters to be jolted into taking on responsibility for themselves and others as a result of some sudden change of fortune or some crisis in their emotional lives and/or physical existences. Scrooge, hero of Dickens's wonderful urban myth, is the great paradigm here, of course, but in the novels we might think, for example, of Nancy suddenly seeing her own pitiable former child-self in Oliver about to be savagely beaten by Fagin and thereafter seeking to save him despite the terrible danger to herself; of Martin Chuzzlewit and his life-changing experience in the swamps of Eden and of David Copperfield forced to become 'a woodcutter in the forest of difficulty' after the apparent ruin of his nurturing aunt; of Louisa Gradgrind arrived at the bottom step of Mrs Sparsit's staircase and Sydney Carton suddenly inspired with a sublimated love for Lucie Manette; of Bella Wilfer, finally revolted by Boffin's seeming brutality towards John Harmon and turning on her apparently degraded patron; and of Eugene Wrayburn, the former pursuer of Lizzie Hexam, lying on what is expected to be his deathbed and murmuring the word 'wife'. And then there are all those young girls featured in the previous chapter who, even in their childish years, assume responsibility for fathers, grandfathers, brothers, sisters or – in default of dependent relatives – their little schoolfellows as Esther Summerson does at the Miss Donnys' (*BH*, 3; of course, Esther soon metamorphoses into 'Dame Durden', the busy chatelaine of Bleak House, and takes on responsibility for a great number of people).

But, as so often, it is in his shorter fiction – his Christmas stories and such like – that Dickens's ideal type appears with cartoon clarity. I am thinking particularly here of Alice Rainbird, the narrator-heroine of one of the supposedly children-authored stories in *Holiday Romance*, written by Dickens in 1868 for an American magazine called *Our Young Folks*. Alice, who bestows 'fanciful' royal titles on herself, her highly polyphiloprogenitive parents and her siblings, describes what she did when her mother became 'very ill indeed, for a long time':

The Princess Alicia kept the seventeen young Princes and Princesses quiet, and dressed and undressed and danced the baby, and made the kettle boil, and heated the soup, and swept the hearth and poured out the medicine, and nursed the Queen, and did all that ever she could, and was as busy busy busy, as busy could be. For there were not many servants at that Palace, for three reasons; because the King was short of money, because a rise in his office never seemed to come, and because quarter-day was so far off that it looked almost as far off and as little as one of the stars.

Behind this predilection for showing children shouldering the responsibilities of adults it is, of course, easy enough to discern Dickens's searing memory of the figure of his 12-year-old self trudging to the hated blacking factory – thrust into a bleak world of self-dependence, 'so young and childish,' he wrote later, 'and so little qualified – how could it be otherwise? – to undertake the whole charge of my own existence'. He must inevitably have felt, too, that the economic survival of his imprisoned parents, and the family generally, partly depended on himself. It is certainly true that, as soon as he began to make an income as a young reporter, he assumed responsibility for his parents, who were subject to constant Micawberesque 'pecuniary difficulties', and for his younger brothers; and, as his life went on, such 'blood-petitioners' (as he once called his parents) became ever more numerous, his own nine surviving children included. He carried, he wrote in a letter of 11 January 1864, 'as long and as heavy a train of dependents as ever was borne by one working man'. Thanks to his dazzling financial success as a writer, he was able – though not without outbreaks of exasperation and occasional anxiety – to meet these responsibilities and that this was a matter of some pride for him seems clear from a rather disagreeable reference to it in his will:

AND I DESIRE here simply to record the fact that my wife, since our separation by consent, has been in the receipt from me of an annual income of £600, while all the great charges of a numerous and expensive family have devolved wholly upon myself.

Dickens carried his sense of family responsibility even to the length of making provision for the 'widow' of his brother Augustus in Chicago while continuing to support in England the legitimate wife whom Augustus had deserted and who suffered from blindness.

He had also, as mentioned above in connection with his involvement in the 'Dignity of Literature' debate, a keen sense of responsibility towards his fellow artists, his 'order' as he and others would have put it. Eliza Franklin, a young house-guest of the Dickenses in 1840, commented in a letter home that 'his constant Charity is Giving away things to distressed authors' and no one in his day was a more energetic champion of professional workers in the arts, especially writers and actors, than Dickens. As already noted (above, p. 44), he fought long and hard, though in the end without success, to reform and make more effective the Royal Literary Fund, established in 1790 to dispense charity to impoverished writers; he spoke often at fund-raising dinners on behalf of the General Theatrical Fund, set up in 1845 to provide pensions for superannuated members of the acting profession; and in the early 1850s he threw himself into an enormous amount of amateur dramatic activity (both as manager and as leading actor) to raise money for the 'Guild of Literature and Art' that he and his admired friend Sir Edward Bulwer had initiated to provide homes and financial help for impoverished writers and artists (it would, Dickens hoped, 'entirely change the status of the literary man in England').

Above all, Dickens felt, very strongly throughout his whole career, that he had a great – indeed, because of the extraordinary

nature, the durability, and the extent of his popularity, a unique
– public responsibility as a writer. He wished to entertain his
readers, certainly, having always had, as he put it in a speech in
Boston in 1842, 'an earnest and true desire to contribute, as far
as in me lies, to the common stock of healthful cheerfulness and
enjoyment' and this he did supremely well, even if sometimes
it meant writing with what he once described in a letter as
'determined jocularity'. But we have also seen earlier how
strongly he felt the responsibility of doing all in his power to
promote the life of the imagination in all walks of life and in all
classes of society, and so too did he feel an *educational* responsibility which involved making his great public vividly aware
of such evils as Chancery injustices, Poor Law brutalities,
Circumlocution Office obfuscations, and such inveterate obstacles to social progress as the City of London's Court of
Common Council. In August 1854, just after he had finished
writing *Hard Times* (which ends with an exhortation to the
individual reader to take on personal responsibility for promot-
ing social good in his or her sphere of action), he wrote to an
American correspondent about one of his guiding lights as a
novelist:

> To interest and affect the general mind in behalf of
> anything that is clearly wrong – to stimulate and rouse the
> public soul to a compassionate or indignant feeling that
> *it must not be* – without obtruding any pet theory of cause
> or cure, and so throwing off allies as they spring up – I
> believe to be one of Fiction's highest uses. And this is the
> use to which I try to turn it. (24 Aug. 1854)

There writes the man whose face, according to his friend the
Hon. Mrs Watson of Rockingham Castle, 'used to *blaze* with
indignation at any injustice or cruelty, and be awful, almost,
over horrors'. But Dickens was also concerned, on the positive
side, to make his readers happily aware of all hopeful signs of

social progress and of all beneficent developments in technology – the railway, for example, 'trailing smoothly away, upon its mighty course of civilisation and improvement' (*DS*, 6) – as well as of all the good so often quietly and unostentatiously done by ordinary people. A good example of such well-doing was the Welsh clergyman who had the responsibility of dealing with the consequences of an appalling shipwreck on his local coast and who

> ... buried many scores of the shipwrecked people ... opened his house and heart to their agonised friends [and] used a most sweet and patient diligence for weeks and weeks, in the performance of the forlornest offices that Man can render to his kind. (*UT*, 'The Shipwreck')

Dickens seems always to have been very conscious – how could he not have been? – of his special role as England's best-loved novelist whose satirical attacks on wrong-doers and incompetents ('incapables' and 'imbeciles', to use his own favourite words for the latter group) were very widespread in their effect, as were his celebrations of human love and goodness, and he seems to have been very conscious, too, of the responsibilities that went with this status. When, for example, it began to seem, in the autumn of 1847, that the pressure of writing *Dombey and Son* would prevent him from producing a Christmas Book that year in the way that he had regularly done since Christmas 1843, he wrote to Forster that he was 'very loath to lose the money' but added that he was 'still more so to leave any gap at Christmas firesides *which I ought to fill*' (my italics). And it was in writing *Dombey* that he hesitated over his notion of showing young Walter Gay 'gradually and naturally trailing away, from that love of adventure and boyish light-heartedness, into negligence, idleness, dissipation, dishonesty and ruin' because, even though 'it might be made very powerful and very useful', it might make readers 'angry' which would have tended to negate its moral 'usefulness'. (It seems from what Forster writes that it was he who persuaded Dickens, for unspecified reasons, perhaps rather more commercial ones, not to follow through with this idea.)

It was, I believe, this strong sense of responsibility towards his public as much as any more turbulent emotion that, in 1858, caused Dickens to take the sensational and very ill-advised step of publicising his marital difficulties in the press, in the same statement repudiating the scandalous rumours that had begun to circulate about his sex life. Having recalled that he had 'entered on [his] present relations with the Public' nearly a quarter of a century earlier, Dickens continues:

> Through all that time I have tried to be as faithful to the Public, as they have been to me. It was my duty never to trifle with them, or deceive them, or presume upon their favour, or do any thing but work hard to justify it. I have always endeavoured to discharge that duty. ('Personal', *HW*, 12 June 1859)

He writes here, we notice, more like a conscientious civil servant, an anti Mr Tite Barnacle (*LD*), proud of his long record of devoted public service, than like a great artist, the 'uncanny genius' that his younger daughter so aptly termed him.

If there was one section of the British public towards which Dickens felt a very special responsibility it was the teeming poor of England, Wales and Scotland (like so many of his contemporaries, including his close friend, Douglas Jerrold of *Punch* fame, the so-called 'people's champion', he seems to have had something of a blind spot when it came to Ireland): 'I take it', he said in 1842, in the course of his famous 'International Copyright' speech in Hartford, Connecticut, 'that we hold our sympathies, hopes and energies in trust for the many, and not for the few'. This sense of responsibility towards the masses generally expresses itself in very paternalistic terms, which no doubt gave an extra edge to Dickens's satire (in *The Chimes*, 1844) on those for whom such paternalism was merely a matter of political rhetoric. Haranguing Trotty Veck the hapless ticket-porter (licensed street-messenger), Sir Joseph Bowley, M.P., the self-styled 'Poor Man's Friend', orates as follows:

> ... your only business in life is with me. You needn't trouble yourself to think about anything. I will think for you; I know what is good for you; I am your perpetual parent. Such is the dispensation of an all-wise Providence! Now, the design of your creation is ... that you should feel the Dignity of Labour. Go forth erect into the cheerful morning air, and – and stop there. Live hard and temperately, be respectful, exercise your self-denial, bring up your family on next to nothing, pay your rent as regularly as the clock strikes, be punctual in your dealings ... and you may trust to me to be your Friend and Father.

Trotty's great error is to allow himself to be persuaded by newspaper reports of crimes committed by the poor that people of his class must be 'born bad'. In *The Chimes* and in many other writings Dickens argues that the only responsibility towards Trotty and his class that the State seems to recognise is that of punishing them when they transgress by locking them up in gaols (others are herded into those 'Poor Law Bastilles', the workhouses) or by hanging them on the gallows. The rural labourer Will Fern appears as a jailbird in the harrowing vision of a likely future Trotty is made to experience, and pleads with Sir Joseph and his friends:

> Gentlemen, gentlemen, dealing with other men like me, begin at the right end. Give us, in mercy better homes when we're a-lying in our cradles; give us better food when we're a-working for our lives; give us kinder laws

to bring us back when we're a-going wrong; and don't set Jail, Jail, Jail, afore us, everywhere we turn.

If their rulers were to do this, to be genuinely and benignly paternalistic, then, says Fern, the labouring classes would be docile and grateful; continued harsh punishment of the poor just for being poor can lead to nothing but the making of more criminals. Two decades later Dickens's most famous jailbird, Magwitch, sums up his life-story for Pip and Herbert in 'a mouthful of English': 'In jail and out of jail, in jail and out of jail, in jail and out of jail. There, you've got it' (*GE*, 42).

Four years after the appearance of *The Chimes* (which occasioned the Chartist newspaper *The Northern Star* to claim rejoicingly, 'Mr DICKENS enters the public arena, as the champion of the poor!') Dickens wrote a life of Jesus for his children (never intended for publication) in which he seeks to communicate to them his sense of personal and class responsibility towards the poor:

> If they are bad, think that they would have been better, if they had had kind friends, and good homes, and had been better taught. So, always try to make them better by kind persuading words; and always try to teach them and relieve them if you can. (ch. 3)

In his fiction, his journalism and his public activities he campaigned tirelessly for better housing, better sanitary conditions, and better educational provision for the working classes whilst in his private life he was remarkably generous towards individuals who asked him for help (to say nothing of all his years of devoted work for Miss Coutts's 'Home for Homeless Women'). Inevitably, he became a prime target for practitioners of the squalid trade of begging-letter writing, as he wryly lamented in an *HW* article on 18 May 1850 ('For fourteen years, my house has been made as regular a receiving House for such communications as any one of the great branch Post-Offices is for general correspondence … ') but he seems never to have let this deter him from trying to help in all cases of genuine distress.

It was towards the children of the poor especially that Dickens felt the strongest sense of responsibility and once he had broken through to a huge readership, following the 'skyrocket' success of *Pickwick*, he took every opportunity, from *Oliver Twist* onwards, to bring the plight of these children, and the social danger that they represented, to the attention of the middle-class public as strikingly as possible. He played, as do the Ghosts in the *Carol* in their conversion of Scrooge, on the emotions of pity and fear and he used all means open to him – fiction, journalism and public speeches. Horrified by the terrible revelations regarding the exploitation of child labour in the *Second Report* ('Trades and Manufactures') of the Children's Employment Commission, he wrote (6 March 1843) to one of the commissioners, Dr Southwood Smith, to say that he was thinking of publishing 'a very cheap pamphlet, called "An appeal to the People of England, on behalf of the Poor Man's Child" – with my name attached, of course'. This project was deferred and eventually subsumed in the writing of the *Carol*, in which Scrooge, confronted with two terrible little child-figures ('wretched, abject, frightful, hideous, miserable'), receives a dire warning:

This boy is Ignorance. This girl is Want. Beware them both, and all of their degree, but most of all beware this boy, for on his brow I see that written which is Doom, unless the writing be erased.

Dickens has broadened the scope of his 'Appeal' in that his text does not present Ignorance and Want as exploited factory children, though the topical theme is still hinted at in Leech's illustration of the scene which shows factory-like buildings and tall chimneys in the background.

In the *Carol* there appears for the first time in Dickens's fictional writings a sympathetic non-comic male child character who is genuinely a child of the poor (the only exception I can think of is the rather insubstantial – in more senses than one – figure of Little Dick in *Oliver Twist*). In the earlier fiction there is no male equivalent of the wonderful shrewd little Marchioness in *The Old Curiosity Shop*. Instead, we have the figures of Oliver and Smike, both conceived in terms of a certain tried and tested configuration of melodrama. They are déclassé rather than genuine children of the poor, as if Dickens himself was still too traumatised by his own 'hard experiences in boyhood' to be able to present this figure as anything other than a middle-class child who has been deprived of his heritage by the sins of the parents. At this stage it is only within the format of a Christmas ghost-story that he can present sympathetically a genuine male child of the poor, stressing either pathos, as in the case of the especially vulnerable Tiny Tim, or horror as in the case of the ferocious street-child in *The Haunted Man*, no longer an allegorical presence like Ignorance and Want but a real 'baby monster'. The grim Phantom (a sort of fetch of himself) that haunts the Haunted Man points up the responsibility of every respectable citizen in the country for 'this wretched mortal [who] from his birth has been abandoned to a worse condition than the beasts':

> There is not a father … by whose side in his daily or nightly walk, these creatures pass; there is not a mother among all the ranks of loving mothers in this land; there is no one risen from the state of childhood, but shall be responsible in his or her degree for this enormity. There is not a country throughout the earth on which it would not bring a curse. There is no religion upon earth it would

not deny; there is no people upon earth it would not put to shame.

Years later, in his 'Uncommercial Traveller' essays, Dickens reminds his readers that these children have not gone away. They still 'prowl about' Covent Garden,

> ... sleep in the baskets, fight for the offal, dart at any object they think they can lay their thieving hands on, dive under the carts and barrows, dodge the constables, and are perpetually making a blunt pattering on the pavement of the Piazza with the rain of their naked feet. (*UT* 'Night Walks', 21 July 1860)

They pervade the streets of London and when (as described in a later essay) the Uncommercial accidentally knocks one of them down and stops to pick it up,

> ... fifty like it, but of both sexes, were about me in a moment, begging, tumbling, fighting, clamouring, yelling, shivering in their nakedness and hunger. The piece of money I had put into the claw of the child I had overturned was clawed out of it, and was clawed out of that wolfish gripe, and again out of that, and soon I had no notion in what part of the obscene scuffle in the mud, of rags and legs and arms and dirt, the money might be. ('On an Amateur Beat', 1869)

A representative of these street-children did not appear in his major fiction until after *David Copperfield*. The story of David's sufferings as a 'little labouring hind' at Murdstone and Grinby's warehouse, came so close to the actual facts of Dickens's own experience, that it seems finally to have exorcised the figure of 'the young gentleman' made to paste labels on blacking bottles in Warren's factory (the monthly number-plan describing little David in the warehouse has only one simple and poignant 'mem.'; it reads: 'What I know so well'). This 'exorcism' certainly paved the way for the creation of Pip in *Great Expectations* but, more immediately, it allowed for the presentation of the main poor-child figure in the next novel *Bleak House* as a genuine, if somewhat sentimentalised, child of the slums. Jo the crossings-sweeper is rooted in Dickens's social journalism rather than in his biography. Only a month or so before introducing the character into *Bleak House*, for example, Dickens had written a piece describing a Ragged School that was also used as a night-sanctuary for homeless boys and men, and in it he painted a haunting picture of a poor child *in extremis* which finds a reflection in the portrayal of Jo after he falls sick, 'an orphan boy with burning cheeks and great gaunt eager eyes, who was in pressing peril of death ... and who had no possession under the broad sky but a bottle of physic and a scrap of writing' ('A Sleep To Startle Us'; *HW*, 13 March 1852). In the novel Dickens powerfully dramatises the shameful neglect or mistreatment of Jo by both secular and religious authorities when he has the boy admire the size of the building that houses the Society for the Propagation of the Gospel in Foreign Parts and '[wonder] what it's all about', having, Dickens sardonically observes, 'no idea of the spiritual desolation of a coral reef in the Pacific'. In the brutally stupid way in which oxen are driven into Smithfield market (always a scene of horror for him) Dickens sees an image of the way the English poor are misgoverned:

> The blinded oxen, over-goaded, over-driven, never guided, run into wrong places and are beaten out; and plunge, red-eyed and foaming, at stone walls; and often sorely hurt the innocent, and often sorely hurt themselves. Very like Jo and his order; very, very like! (*BH*, 16)

Magwitch, we may remember, tells Pip how as a child and a young man he was 'whipped and worried and drove' until at last he fell into the evil company of Compeyson.

For Dickens it is always a question of neglected duty towards the poorer classes on the part of those in power and those who support them in power, including his own middle-class readers. Phrases about 'owing a duty to society' become a hollow mockery in the mouths of Dickens's bourgeois monsters like Mr Pecksniff or Mr Podsnap and in *Martin Chuzzlewit* he sounds off in Carlylean rhetorical style:

> Oh ermined judge whose duty to society is, now, to doom the ragged criminal to punishment and death, hadst thou never, Man, a duty to discharge in barring up the hundred open gates that wooed him to the felon's dock, and throwing but ajar the portals to a decent life! ... Oh magistrate, so rare a country gentleman and brave a squire, had you no duty to society, before the ricks were blazing and the mob were mad; or did it spring up, armed and booted from the earth, a corps of yeomanry, full-grown! (*MC*, 31)

Twenty years later he is still intent on driving the point home, albeit no longer in the language of melodrama (the Hungry Forties with the overhanging threat of imminent revolution had passed). At the beginning of an essay entitled 'The Short-Timers' (*ATYR*, 20 June 1863) praising the Limehouse Schools of Industry, which had been established for pauper children in the 1840s by the local Poor Law authorities, Dickens muses in his Uncommercial Traveller mode that he can find 'within so many yards of Westminster Abbey, Saint Paul's Cathedral, the Houses of Parliament, the Prisons, the Courts of Justice, all the Institutions that govern the land

... in the open streets, shameful instances of neglect of children, intolerable toleration of the engenderment of paupers, idlers, thieves, races of wretched and destructive cripples both in body and mind, a misery to themselves, a misery to the community, a disgrace to civilisation, and an outrage on Christianity. I know it to be a fact as easy of demonstration as any sum in any of the elementary rules of arithmetic, that if the State would begin its work and duty at the beginning, and would with the strong hand take those children out of the streets, while they are yet children, and wisely train them, it would make them a part of England's glory, not its shame ... would raise good soldiers and sailors, and good citizens, and many great men, out of the seeds of its criminal population.

The initiative of the Limehouse authorities had achieved something on a local scale, just as the work of charities like the East London Hospital for Children and the Great Ormond Street Hospital for Sick Children provided opportunities to celebrate pin-points of light in the darkness. It was on behalf of Great Ormond Street that Dickens made in 1858 perhaps the finest of all the great speeches he made at fund-raising dinners during over thirty years of public speaking (he also featured the Hospital in *Our Mutual Friend*). In his speech he recalled a sick infant he had once seen in an Edinburgh slum:

... where there was an empty porridge-pot on the cold hearth, with a ragged woman and some ragged children crouching on the bare ground near it – there lay, in an old egg-box which the mother had begged from a shop, a little feeble, wasted, wan, sick child. With his little wasted face, and his little hot worn hands folded over his breast, and his little bright attentive eyes, I can see him now, as I have seen him for several years, looking steadily at us. There he lay in his little frail box, which was not at all a bad emblem of the little body from which he was slowly parting – there he lay, quite quiet, quite patient, saying never a word. He seldom cried, the mother said; he seldom complained; 'he lay there, seeming to wonder what it was a' aboot'.

Building on this imagined question in the mind of the dying child (which echoes Jo's question about the S.P.G.F.P. building) and the thought of all the children doomed to a similar death, Dickens made such a powerful plea to his audience to give money to support and enlarge the Great Ormond Street Hospital that one lady in the gallery was even moved to write a cheque for as much as £500.

He had been equally fervent a few years earlier in his support for the so-called 'Ragged Schools' which were trying to provide some rudimentary education for at least a handful of London's swarming street-children. He enlisted the help of the millionaire philanthropist, Miss Burdett Coutts by sending her what he called a 'sledge-hammer account' of his visit to the Field Lane School in Saffron Hill, the very neighbourhood in which he had earlier located Fagin's lair:

> I have very seldom seen, in all the strange and dreadful things I have seen in London and elsewhere, anything so shocking as the dire neglect of soul and body exhibited in these children. And, although I know; and am as sure as it is possible for to be of anything which has not happened; that in the prodigious misery and ignorance of the swarming masses of mankind in England, the seeds of its certain ruin are sown, I never saw that Truth so staring out in hopeless characters, as it does from the walls of this place. (16 Sept. 1843)

One would hesitate to say that he was trying, like his own Fat Boy in *Pickwick*, to make Miss Coutts's flesh creep but it is not difficult to see in this report of his Field Lane experience the origin of the conception of Ignorance and Want in the *Carol*, written just a month or so later, and of the apocalyptic warning about impending social catastrophe that the Ghost of Christmas Present delivers to the trembling Scrooge.

With the Ragged Schools, as with the children's hospitals and with emigration societies like Mrs Caroline Chisholm's (helping those who could not find work, or only work for starvation wages, to seek a better life in Australia), Dickens felt that private charitable movements were at least better than nothing so long as Government continued to shirk its responsibilities to the poorer classes, but he was always very much alive to the potential drawbacks of such charities. Educational ones could stigmatise the recipients of their help by making them wear humiliating uniforms that incited other children to torment them in the streets (Noah Claypole in *Oliver Twist* and Robin Toodles in *Dombey and Son* both suffer in this way and this encourages vicious propensities in both of them), they could empower incompetent brutes like the unfortunate Robin's schoolmaster, a 'superannuated old Grinder of savage disposition ... for whose cruel cane all chubby little boys had a perfect fascination'; or they could, by demanding lip-service to certain social or religious ideas, foster hypocrisy like the 'foundation school' and the 'public, sort of charitable, establishment', the places to which the Heep family owes its education (*DC*, ch. 39). Even Miss Coutts, 'excellent creature' as she was in Dickens's eyes, had her 'pet theories' and had sometimes to be gently argued out of them by him in his almoner role so that she may agree, for example, to the girls in Urania Cottage dressing in bright colours rather than in a drearily drab material called 'derry'. With regard to the Ragged Schools he had to tread carefully, on account of Miss Coutts's fervent Anglicanism, in criticising the religious instruction so injudiciously forced on the pupils by well-meaning volunteer teachers. By 1865, however, his relationship with her was more distant and he could paint a devastating picture of such a teacher in Charley Hexam's Ragged School ('a miserable loft in an unsavoury yard'). This teacher, 'the prosiest and worst of all the teachers with good intentions', Dickens describes as 'drawling on' to a 'hot-bed of flushed and exhausted infants' about 'the beautiful coming to the Sepulchre; and repeating the word Sepulchre (commonly used among infants) five hundred times, and never once hinting what it meant' (*OMF*, II. 1).

It is, of course, the Government that Dickens believes should be taking responsibility for the education of these children, as well as for their health and the health of the poor generally. But he did not believe that State intervention was any more proof against bad results than were private charities when it was based upon wrong premises or some 'pet theory' such as that cherished by the Utilitarians. Given his passionate concern for nourishing the life of the imagination, Dickens naturally viewed with a certain amount of horror the work of the Liberal politician Sir James Kay-Shuttleworth, who was from 1839 the first secretary of a Privy Council committee on public education. Kay-Shuttleworth, whose 'supernatural dreariness' made Dickens feel, he once wrote to Miss Coutts, 'as if I had just come out of the Great Desert of Sahara where my camel died a fortnight ago' (1 April 1853), laid great emphasis on the acquiring and imparting of factual knowledge and this was strongly reflected in the syllabus of the Government-funded Training Colleges for teachers that he established. Dickens's view of this situation is sufficiently indicated in his depiction of the satirical-cartoon figure of the Utilitarian schoolmaster, Mr M'Choakumchild (*HT*, I. 1.) and the far more complexly rendered figure of the tormented National School teacher Bradley Headstone (*OMF*), both of them supposedly products of the Kay-Shuttleworthian system.

Generally, however, it is for failing in its responsibilities to the country as a whole, especially with regard to the more vulnerable section of its population, that Dickens attacks

Parliament. M.P.s from *Sketches by Boz* onwards invariably cut a poor figure in his writings. They seem more concerned with their own importance – like Cornelius Brook Dingwall, fatuously preoccupied with removing the duty on beeswax or his 'Bill for the better observance of Easter Monday' (*SB*, 'Sentiment'), or the egregious Mr Gregsbury in *Nicholas Nickleby* (ch. 16) – or else with their own party-political games (like the professional games played by the lawyers in *Bleak House*) than with any serious attempt to improve social conditions. Even that well-meaning social theorist Mr Gradgrind is described after becoming an M.P. as merely having become one of 'the national dustmen' whose chief occupation it is to 'entertain one another with a great many noisy little fights among themselves' (*HT*, II.11). David Copperfield's jaundiced view from the reporters' gallery in the Commons of those whom Dickens calls, in a letter of 28 February 1852, 'the bellowers and prosers of St Stephens' has always been taken, and with good reason, to be pretty directly autobiographical:

> Night after night, I record predictions that never come to pass, professions that are never fulfilled, explanations that are only meant to mystify. I wallow in words. Britannia, that unfortunate female is always before me, like a trussed fowl: skewered through and through with office pens, and bound hand and foot in red tape. I am sufficiently behind the scenes to know the worth of political life. I am quite an infidel about it and shall never be converted. (*DC*, 43)

Certainly Dickens himself consistently refused all invitations to stand for Parliament, preferring, as he put it in 1852, 'to be as useful [i. e., to the nation] as I can in my own way'. His 'own way' included describing with the use of much powerful imagery – 'fancy' in the service of social reform – the shameful squalor and degradation of the London slums in such a fashion as to rouse the national conscience in a way that Parliamentary speechifying or campaigning on behalf of this or that pressure group never could. He points to the ineffectiveness of such speech-making in his description of that 'black, dilapidated street, avoided by all decent people' known as 'Tom-All-Alone's' in *Bleak House*:

> Much mighty speech-making there has been, both in and out of Parliament, concerning Tom, and much wrathful disputation how Tom shall be got right. Whether he shall be put into the main road by constables, or by beadles, or by bell-ringing, or by force of figures, or by correct principles of taste, or by high church, or by low church, or by no church; ... In the midst of which dust and noise, there is but one thing perfectly clear, to wit, that Tom only may and can, or shall and will, be reclaimed according to somebody's theory but nobody's practice. And in the hopeful meantime, Tom goes to petition head foremost in his old determined spirit. (*BH*, 46)

Dickens's general contempt for what his revered friend Carlyle scornfully dismissed as 'the National Palaver' did not prevent him from admiring and respecting some individual M.P.s, notably Lord John Russell, twice Prime Minister, with whom he was on friendly terms and of whose energetic dedication, both in and out of office, to political, sanitary and educational reform he highly approved. Russell must have seemed to him the ideal dedicatee for *A Tale of Two Cities*, his French Revolution novel with its clear warning to 1860's England about the huge social catastrophe that could overcome a country when its ruling classes abandoned themselves to criminal irresponsibility and perpetrated massive social injustice:

> Crush humanity out of shape once more, under similar hammers, and it will twist itself into the same tortured

forms. Sow the same seed of rapacious license and oppression over again, and it will surely yield the same fruit
according to its kind. (*TTC*, III.15)

Dickens also strongly approved of the great archaeologist,
Layard of Nineveh, who became an M.P. in 1852 and who,
three years later, called the Government to account for the gross
misconduct and hideous débacle of the Crimean War. Layard
was a moving spirit of the Administrative Reform Association,
the only political movement that Dickens ever joined, and for
which he made a powerful speech in June 1855, just as he
was beginning to write *Little Dorrit* (originally entitled, with
contemptuous reference to governmental shirking of responsibility, 'Nobody's Fault'). Explaining in this speech why he had
joined the Association, Dickens said:

> I want at all times, in full sincerity, to do my duty by my
> countrymen ... . In my sphere of action I have tried to
> understand the heavier social grievances, and to help set
> them right ... . With the machinery of Government and
> the legislature going round and round, and the people
> fallen from it and standing aloof, as if they left it to its last
> remaining function of destroying itself, when it had
> achieved the destruction of so much that was dear to them
> − I did and do believe that the only wholesome turn
> affairs so menacing could possibly take, was, the awak-
> ening of the people ... the uniting of the people to effect
> a great peaceful constitutional change in the administra-
> tion of their own affairs. At such a crisis this association
> arose; at such a crisis I joined it ... .

The speech echoes his leading *HW* article of a few months
earlier, 'To Working Men', which had been prompted by the
outbreak of another cholera epidemic in London. In this Dickens

had pointed out that he was simply continuing a campaign that he had begun many years earlier:

> Long before this Journal came into existence, we systematically tried to turn Fiction to the good account of showing the preventable wretchedness and misery in which the mass of the people dwell [he might have instanced here his famous description of the hideous slum called 'Jacob's Island' in *Oliver Twist* ch. 50], and of expressing again and again the conviction, founded upon observation, that the reform of their habitations must precede all other reforms; and that without it, all other reforms must fail. Neither Religion nor Education will make any way, in this nineteenth century of Christianity, until a Christian government shall have discharged its first obligation, and secured to the people Homes, instead of polluted dens.

Dickens was decidedly vague about just how the working men he is (somewhat indirectly) addressing in this piece might go about enforcing such a desirable change of government but, being a Smilesian self-help man in political matters as in much else, he made it clear that he considered the responsibility for doing so was primarily theirs:

> ... the movement, to be irresistible, must originate with themselves, the suffering many. Let them take the initiative, and call the middle-class to unite with them: which they will do, heart and soul! Let the working people, in the metropolis, in any one great town, but turn their intelligence, their energy, their numbers, their power of union, their patience, their perseverance, in this straight direction in earnest – and by Christmas they shall find a government in Downing-street and a House of Commons within hail of it, possessing not the faintest family resem-

blance to the Indifferents and Incapables last heard of in that slumberous neighbourhood.

No such unlikely change of government having occurred by Christmas 1854, it was left to concerned members of the middle-classes to set up a few months later the Administrative Reform Association.

Dickens did not content himself with making an eloquent speech to the Association. He went on in the writing of *Little Dorrit* scathingly to satirise, through his presentation of Lord Decimus Tite Barnacle and his endlessly-ramifying family, and through the concept of the Circumlocution Office, all the pompously incompetent or frivolously irresponsible politicians and civil servants whom he saw as being to blame for so much grievous mess and muddle in the nation's life. And he has the same targets in his sights in many polemical and satirical pieces written for *Household Words* throughout the 1850s. Chief object of his detestation was that great political survivor, the septuagenarian Lord Palmerston, three times Prime Minister, who with his 'dandy insolence' and consummate skill in party-political games (one of Dickens's offensive names for him is 'Twirling Weathercock') may be said to have embodied everything that Dickens really hated about so many of the aristocratic professional politicians of his day, all those Lord Coodles and Lord Doodles who seemed to regard the people very much as 'supernumeraries' on the political stage, 'to be occasionally addressed, and relied upon for shouts and choruses, as on the theatrical stage' (*BH*, ch. 12) but to whom they were in no sense responsible. Palmerston's notorious jocoseness Dickens found particularly enraging, given the – as he saw it – desperate state of the nation, and in his *HW* journalism he constantly lampoons the old statesman as a superannuated joker. For example, in one (very funny) three-part satire written as a parody of the *Arabian Nights*, 'The Thousand and One Humbugs', he causes Palmerston to describe himself (in the character of the 'Talkative Barber') as

> ... an accomplished diplomat, a first-rate statesman, a frisky speaker, an easy shaver, a touch-and-go joker, a giver of the go-by to all complainers, and above all a member of the aristocracy of Barbers. (*HW*, 5 May 1855)

Whatever else Palmerston was in Dickens's eyes he was certainly not 'earnest', a word that Carlyle with his Schiller-motto, 'Ernst ist das Leben', had taught the Victorians to hold in the highest estimation and that Wilde so devastatingly mocked in his great and glittering comedy five years before the century's end. In Dickens 'earnestness' always underpins responsibility but he also uses the word, like his contemporaries, to express emotional honesty and energy. Oliver Twist has 'a warm and earnest heart', for example, and Dickens never ceased to marvel at 'the most extraordinary earnestness' of his own passionate love for Maria Beadnell in his young manhood. This is reflected, as he later told Maria herself, in the story of young David Copperfield's love for Dora and indeed, as the epigraph at the head of this chapter makes clear, he conceives of 'earnestness' as the very bedrock of David's character, as it is of the book's 'true heroine' and David's eventual wife, Agnes Wickfield. Other leading characters portray variations on the theme. Earnestness is what David's boyhood hero, the brilliantly-gifted Steerforth, so tragically lacks whilst in the single-minded self-advancement by underhand and unscrupulous means practised by David's dark alter ego, Uriah Heep, we see a horribly perverted version of the quality. Even Mr Micawber, that glorious embodiment of benign irresponsibility, becomes very earnest indeed when he finds himself brought into direct contact with evil in the form of the criminal machinations of Uriah (rather as Charley Bates turns honest when confronted with the sheer evil of Sikes's murder of Nancy): he describes the process in his own inimitable epistolary prose (happily unaffected by his moral development):

> Stimulated by the silent monitor within, and by a no less touching and appealing monitor without—to whom I will briefly refer as Miss W — I entered on a not unlaborious task of clandestine investigation, protracted now, to the best of my knowledge, information, and belief, over a period exceeding twelve calendar months. (*DC*, 52)

And, later on, we have Mr Peggotty's charming tribute to the continued earnestness of Mr Micawber when he 'turned to' to make a new life for himself and his family in the Australian bush:

> I never wish to meet a better gen'l'man for turning to, with a will. I've seen that theer bald head of his, a perspiring in the sun, Mas'r Davy, 'till I a'most thowt it would have melted away. And now he's a Magistrate. (*DC*, 63)

In *Bleak House*, the novel that followed *Copperfield*, appears Richard Carstone, another study — in somewhat less Byronic mode than Steerforth — of a young man fatally lacking in those qualities of perseverance and strenuous application which for Dickens are at the very core of true earnestness (his portrait of Richard has sometimes been related to anxiety about his eldest son, Charley, who had turned 17 in 1854 and had, wrote Dickens to Miss Coutts, 'less fixed purpose and energy than I could have supposed possible in a child of mine'). Richard drifts nonchalantly from one profession to another, seemingly unable to devote himself to any of them — a great contrast, as Mrs Bayham Badger the wife of one of his intended mentors observes, to her two distinguished previous husbands, the late Captain Swosser, R. N., whose maxim was 'that if you only have to swab a plank, you should swab it as if Davy Jones were after you', and the late Professor Dingo ('of European reputation') who kept his little geological hammer under his pillow even on his death-bed 'when (his mind wandering) he insisted on … chipping at the countenances of the attendants' (*BH*, 17). When eventually Richard does devote himself to a cause, the hopelessly forlorn one of bringing to a successful conclusion the fatal Chancery suit in which he and Ada are enmeshed, it is, in fact, a question of yielding to a terrible mania, a sick kind of earnestness, the growth of which Esther Summerson watches with pain and pity:

> … it was so unlike hopefulness, had something so fierce in its determination to be it, was so hungry and eager, and yet so conscious of being forced and unsustainable, that it had long touched me to the heart. (*BH*, 51)

We meet mania again in Dickens's next novel *Hard Times* in the form of Mr Gradgrind's obsession with facts and figures as he goes about 'gauging fathomless deeps with his little mean excise-rod and … staggering over the universe with his rusty stiff-legged compasses'. Gradgrind's mania has disastrous public consequences as well as terrible ones for his children but even more dangerous to the world than such horribly misguided earnestness is the complete lack of any earnestness at all in men like the polished, charming and socially privileged James Harthouse with whom Gradgrind's party wants to make a Parliamentary alliance ('The not being troubled with earnestness was a grand point in his favour, enabling him to take to the hard Fact fellows with as good a grace as if he had been born one of the tribe … '). Even when he is drifting towards the seduction of Louisa, wretchedly married to Bounderby as a result of her father's 'system', Harthouse 'had not … any earnest wickedness of purpose in him' and Dickens comments:

Publicly and privately, it were much better for the age in which he lived, that he and the legion of whom he was one were designedly bad, than indifferent and purposeless. It is the drifting icebergs setting without current anywhere that wreck the ships.

When the Devil goeth about like a roaring lion, he goeth about in a shape by which few but savages and hunters are attracted. But when he is trimmed, smoothed, and varnished, according to the mode; when he is aweary of vice and aweary of virtue, used up as to brimstone, and used up as to bliss; then, whether he takes to the serving out of red tape, or to the kindling of red fire, he is the very Devil. (*HT*, II.8)

In his later novels Dickens continues to make the exploration and exemplification of varieties of earnestness and lack of earnestness a prominent feature; the type represented by Harthouse, for example, is redeemed in the development of the equally well-born (as his first name indicates) Eugene Wrayburn in *Our Mutual Friend* who changes from being a prototype Wildean dandy to a husband who will justify his wife's belief that he 'has a mine of purpose and energy and will turn it to the best account' ('In turning to at last, we turn to in earnest', Eugene tells his friend Mortimer who has shared with him in his idleness). Dickens also portrays many more examples of perverted or 'mania' type earnestness, such as Miss Havisham's scheme for revenging herself on the male sex, Bradley Headstone's obsessive desire for Lizzie Hexam (*OMF*) and Jasper's for Rosa Budd in *Edwin Drood*. This kind of earnestness, concerned only with gratifying personal desires, regardless of the consequences for those who may be the object of, or the means of achieving, these desires, is evil whereas Magwitch's earnestness in amassing a fortune has a revenge motive comparable to Miss Havisham's but is essentially benign because it is primarily inspired by gratitude towards, and love for, his 'dear boy'.

The extent to which such studies as the obsessive lovers, Bradley Headstone and John Jasper, in the later fiction relate to the situation in Dickens's own personal life from 1857/58 has been much debated and it is no part of my purpose here to venture out onto that Serbonian bog where so many books have sunk. Still, in any discussion of the theme of earnestness and responsibility towards others in Dickens's later work, it would be strange to make no mention of the way in which, in both his private and his public writings in the latter part of 1857 (he had got to know Ellen that summer when she, her mother and her sister had performed with his amateur company in Manchester), he often seems to be under some sort of compulsion to register a particularly powerful sense of his own extraordinary capacity for earnestness in love. He himself would doubtless have related it to a trait in his character about which he had written to his wife four years earlier, that 'intense pursuit of any idea that takes complete possession of me', one of the qualities, he told her, 'that makes me different — sometimes for good; sometimes I dare say for evil – from other men' (5 Dec. 1853). Writing now to his dear friend, the Hon. Mrs Watson, he expresses his love-earnestness 'fancifully' (she was not, presumably, intended to speculate on a possible real-life identity for the Princess):

I wish I had been born in the days of Ogres and Dragon-guarded Castles. I wish an Ogre with seven heads … had taken the Princess whom I adore – you have no idea how intensely I love her! – to his stronghold on the top of high series of mountains, and there tied her up by the hair. Nothing would suit me half so well this day, as climbing after her, sword in hand, and either winning her or being killed. (7 Dec. 1857)

Two months earlier he had expressed it in a more direct way to his public. He wrote jointly with Wilkie Collins a lightly fictionalised account, published serially in *Household Words*, of a trip to Cumberland that the two had made in September (the northern destination chosen was not unconnected with an engagement that Mrs Ternan and her daughters had to act in Doncaster during Races Week). Borrowing its central device from Hogarth's *Industry and Idleness*, the serialised travelogue is entitled 'The Lazy Tour of Two Idle Apprentices' and a running joke is that one of the 'apprentices', Francis Goodchild (i.e., Dickens), is anything but 'idle', is indeed incapable of being in such a state, especially when in love. He expostulates with Thomas Idle (Collins) over the ballad 'Annie Laurie' which Idle has just been warbling:

> 'What an ass that fellow was!' cried Goodchild, with the bitter emphasis of contempt.
> 'Which fellow?' asked Thomas Idle.
> 'The fellow in your song. Lay him doon and dee! Finely he'd show off before the girl by doing that. A Sniveller! Why couldn't he get up, and punch somebody's head?'
> 'Whose?' asked Thomas Idle.
> 'Anybody's. Everybody's would be better than nobody's! If I fell into that state of mind about a girl, do you think I'd lay me doon and dee? No, sir,' proceeded Goodchild with a disparaging assumption of the Scottish accent, 'I'd get me oop and peetch into somebody. Wouldn't you?'

And later on he mocks his own super-earnestness in everything (whilst at the same time subtly boasting of it, of course) by causing Thomas Idle to reproach him (possibly a version of something that Collins did actually say to him):

'To me you are an absolutely terrible fellow. You do nothing like another man. Where another fellow would fall into a footbath of action or emotion, you fall into a mine. Where any other fellow would be a painted butter-fly, you are a fiery dragon. Where another man would stake a sixpence, you stake your existence. If you were to go up in a balloon, you would make for Heaven: and if you were to dive into the depths of the earth, nothing short of the other place would content you. What a fellow you are, Francis!'

The cheerful Goodchild laughed.

It seems fitting to end this chapter with reference to 'The Lazy Tour' because it is in that story that we find, a few paragraphs after the passage just quoted, Dickens's most deso-lating image of earnestness, but one that he offers as a suitable emblem for the human condition. Mr Goodchild visits the lunatic asylum in Lancaster and there notices

... a poor little dark-skinned, meagre man, with a per-plexed brow and a pensive face, stooping low over the matting on the floor, and picking out with his thumb and fore-finger the course of the fibres.

Oblivious to everything around him, the little man continues to pore over his bit of matting and always returns to doing so whenever he is gently persuaded to desist and find some other occupation. Goodchild, thinking that 'probably the course of those fibres as they plaited in and out, over and under, was the only course of things in the whole wide world that it was left to him to understand', wonders if the man looked into the matting

... to see if it could show him anything of the process through which he came to be there, so strangely poring over it. Then, I thought how all of us, GOD help us! in our different ways are poring over our bits of matting, blindly enough, and what confusions and mysteries we make in the pattern. I had a sadder fellow-feeling with the little dark-chinned, meagre man, by that time, and I came away.

Progress

Good God, the greatest mystery in all the earth, to me, is
how or why the world was tolerated by its Creator
through the good old times, and wasn't dashed to frag-
ments.

Forster, V. 3

And let us not remember Italy the less regardfully, because, in every fragment of her fallen Temples, and every
stone of her deserted palaces and prisons, she helps to
inculcate the lesson that the wheel of Time is rolling for
an end, and that the world is, in all essentials, better,
gentler, more forbearing, and more hopeful, as it rolls!

Concluding words of Pictures from Italy (1846)

We seek to bring into innumerable homes, from the
stirring world around us, the knowledge of many social
wonders ... not calculated to render any of us ... less
thankful for the privilege of living in this summer-dawn
of time.

'A Preliminary Word', Household
Words, 30 March 1850

There is a delightful moment at the end of one of Dickens's
early sketches, 'The River' (SB; first published June 1835),
when some shy paterfamiliases, taking their families on an
outing aboard one of the Saturday steamboats plying from
London Bridge to Gravesend or Margate, are relieved to find

that the boat's engine provides them with a 'copious' subject for some casual chat:

> 'Wonderful thing, steam, sir.' 'Ah! (a deep-drawn sigh) it is indeed, sir.' 'Great power, sir.' 'Immense – immense!' 'Great deal done by steam, sir.' 'Ah! (another sigh at the immensity of the subject, and a knowing shake of the head) you may say that, sir.' 'Still in its infancy, they say, sir.'

It is not difficult to catch occasional echoes of this innocent enthusiasm in the voice of Dickens himself later on, when he touches on the spectacular advances in technology being achieved in his day, what he calls in a letter to Wills of 22 August 1851 'the great progress of the century' (he specifies 'Railway construction ... Electric Telegraph discovery ... improvements in Machinery'). They are to be heard, for example, in a virtuoso piece called 'A Flight' published in *Household Words* just eight days after he had written the letter just quoted. In this essay Dickens celebrates the wondrous fact that the journey from London to Paris now takes only half the time that it did in the not-so-remote days of stage-coaches and French diligences with all their attendant discomforts ('Where are the two-and-twenty hours of long long day and night journey, sure to be either insupportably hot or insupportably cold? ... where is the Frenchman with the nightcap who ... always fell upon me when he went to sleep, and always slept all night snoring onions?'). The echoes can be heard also in the presentation of Mr Rouncewell, the Ironmaster (i. e., manufacturer) in *Bleak House*, when he talks to the majestically displeased Sir Leicester Dedlock (stuck fast in feudal times) of how he needs to be constantly 'on the flight' in 'these busy times, when so many great undertakings are in progress' (*BH*, 28). One can see why John Ruskin, writing to the American scholar Charles Eliot Norton a few days after Dickens's death called him 'a pure modernist – a leader of the steam-whistle party *par excellence*' whose hero was 'essentially the ironmaster'. It is certainly true that Mr Rouncewell is presented in a highly favourable light as he enters the Dedlocks' great drawing-room at Chesney Wold:

> He is a little over fifty perhaps, of a good figure ...; and has a clear voice, a broad forehead from which his dark hair has retired, and a shrewd though open face. He is a responsible-looking gentleman dressed in black, portly enough, but strong and active. Has a perfectly natural and easy air, and is not in the least embarrrassed by the great presence into which he comes.

Unlike the dubious capitalists in *Our Mutual Friend* (1. 10) who traffic in shares and 'oscillate on mysterious business between London and Paris' (one of them, called, simply, 'Monied Interest', appears in 'A Flight'), Mr Rouncewell does actually produce something real and tangible, and something that is fundamental to the technological progress of the age. Dickens's description of Rouncewell's foundry, seen through the eyes of his simple soldier-brother, George, is both bewildering and exhilarating (as well as exhilarated):

> ... a great perplexity of iron lying about, in every stage, and in a vast variety of shapes; in bars, in wedges, in sheets; in tanks, in boilers, in axles, in wheels, in cogs, in cranks, in rails; twisted and wrenched into eccentric and perverse forms, as separate parts of machinery; mountains of it broken up, and rusty in its age; distant furnaces of it glowing and bubbling in its youth; bright fireworks of it showering about, under the blows of the steam-hammer ... (*BH*, 63)

We might compare this with the equally vivid description of the construction of a major London railway terminus in *Dombey and Son* (6):

... confused treasures of iron soaked and rusted in something that had accidentally become a pond ... . There were a hundred thousand shapes and substances of incompleteness, wildly mingled out of their places, upside down, burrowing in the earth, aspiring in the air, mouldering in the water, and unintelligible as any dream. Hot springs and fiery eruptions ... lent their contributions of confusion to the scene ... .

In both cases Dickens's imagination is responding strongly to the stimulus of chaotic scenes, much as it does to the teeming, labyrinthine slums or the confusion of Krook's rag-and-bone shop, image of the more deadly confusion of Chancery ('There's no great odds betwixt us. We both grub on in a muddle', says Krook of himself and the Lord Chancellor). But from out of the seeming chaos of the ironworks or the earthquake-like upheaval that, as a result of railway construction, has struck the squalid neighbourhood of Staggs's Gardens (i. e., Camden Town – Dickens's invented name contains a sly joke about speculators in railway stock), there comes, Dickens delights to note, order, efficiency, the betterment of social conditions: 'from the very core of all this dire disorder [the Railway] trailed smoothly away, upon its mighty course of civilisation and improvement' (*DS*, 6). When, several chapters later, the novel's action returns to Staggs's Gardens it, too, has been utterly transformed for the better by the coming of the railway:

Where the old rotten summer-houses once had stood, palaces now reared their heads, and granite columns opened a vista to the railway world beyond. The miserable waste ground, where the refuse-matter had been heaped of yore was swallowed up and gone; and in its frowsy stead were tiers of warehouses, crammed with rich goods and costly merchandise. The old by-streets

now swarmed with passengers and vehicles of every
kind: the new streets that had stopped disheartened in the
mud and waggon-ruts, formed towns within themselves
originating wholesome comforts and conveniences belonging to themselves and never tried nor thought of until
they sprung into existence ... . (*DS*, 15)

For Dickens, as for his contemporaries, the railway was by
far the most obvious, dramatic, and ubiquitous example of the
'progressive' nature of the age. The rapidity of its spread over
the whole country and the profound effect it had on so many
aspects of daily life, beginning with the establishment of 'railway time' throughout the land, made people feel they had been
precipitated into an utterly new world:

> We who have lived before railways were made, belong to
> another world. In how many hours could the Prince of
> Wales drive from Brighton to London, with a light car-
> riage built expressly, and relays of horses longing to
> gallop the next stage? ... . It was only yesterday; but what
> a gulf between then and now! *Then* was the old world.
> Stage-coaches, more or less swift, riding-horses, pack-
> horses, highwaymen, knights in armour, Norman
> invaders, Roman legions, Druids, Ancient Britains
> painted blue, and so forth – all these belong to the old
> period. I will concede a halt in the midst of it and allow
> that gunpowder and printing tended to modernise the
> world. But your railroad starts the new era ... .
>
> (Thackeray, 'De Juventute', *Roundabout Papers*, 1863)

For Dickens, the railway does not only start a new era; it
brings with it a marked increase in the movement towards that
'better, gentler, more forbearing, and more hopeful' world to
which he looks forward at the end of *Pictures From Italy*. He
writes in his 1847 Preface to the Cheap Edition of *Pickwick*

Papers that he has been struck, in re-reading the novel, by the 'important social improvements' that have taken place in England since the time when he launched Mr Pickwick on his stage-coach rambles, and he links these improvements closely with the railways:

> ... places far apart are brought together, to the present convenience and advantage of the Public, and to the certain destruction, in time, of a host of petty jealousies, blindnesses, and prejudices, by which the Public alone have always been the sufferers ... .

The railway engine, speeding on its 'iron way' and 'piercing through the heart of every obstacle', may seem like 'a type of the triumphant monster, Death' to Mr Dombey's engloomed imagination (as much in need of 'sweetening' as the mad King Lear's) but it is, in fact, on the side of life, letting in 'the light of day' (and thus the prospect of sanitary reform) upon the horrible slums 'where want and fever hide themselves in many wretched shapes' (*DS*, 20). There was much about the development of the railways of which Dickens was severely critical, from the irresponsibility of Boards of Directors playing fast and loose with the safety of the public to the surliness of refreshment room staff. Indeed, the aggressively disagreeable woman, fortified behind tea-urns and treating the travelling public as her natural enemy, is a recurrent figure in his writings; she is portrayed at full length in the hilarious 'The Boy at Mugby' (*CS*, 'Mugby Junction', 1866). But towards the railway itself, and the truly marvellous organisation of which it was the result, he had nothing but entirely positive feelings:

> It is the result of a vast system of skilful combination, and a vast expenditure of wealth. The construction of the line alone, against all the engineering difficulties it presented, involved an amount of outlay that was wonderful, even

in England. To bring it to its present state of working efficiency, a thousand ingenious problems have been studied and solved, stupendous machines have been constructed, a variety of plans and schemes have been matured with incredible labour: a great whole has been pieced together by numerous capacities and appliances, and kept incessantly in motion. (*HW*, 'Railway Strikes', 11 Jan. 1851)

In a letter written from Italy a few years earlier (16 Nov. 1844) to his famous journalist friend, Douglas Jerrold, whose social and political attitudes coincided so closely with his own, Dickens cites the coming of the railway to Venice as a great example of enlightened progress. He had inspected with fascinated horror (the 'attraction of repulsion' working at a very intense pitch) the gloomy underwater cells in the prisons of the Doge 'where the Monk came at midnight to confess the political offender' before the latter was strangled. 'These things, ' he wrote to Jerrold, 'stir a man's blood, like a great Wrong or Passion of the Instant'. Yet, despite people's memory of such things and the existence of a museum full of frightful instruments of torture,

... there are hundreds of parrots who will declaim to you in speech and print by the hour together, on the degeneracy of the times in which a Railroad is building across the Water to Venice! Instead of going down on their knees, the drivellers, and thanking Heaven they live in a time when Iron makes Roads instead of Prison Bars, and engines for driving screws into the heads of innocent men.

Visiting Italy again, in 1853, Dickens joyfully notes an equally striking instance of wonderful modern, life-enhancing technology juxtaposed with a grim reminder of the past, of 'ages of darkness, wickedness and violence'. 'The Electric Telegraph', he reports to Forster from Rome, 'now goes like a sunbeam through the cruel old heart of the Coliseum' (Forster, VII. 3). On his first visit to Rome Dickens's imagination had been deeply stirred by the Coliseum (or 'Colosseum' as we now spell it); he had a powerful vision of it as it had been 'in its bloodiest prime' with 'thousands of eager faces staring down into the arena, and such a whirl of strife, and blood, and dust going on there as no language can describe'; and he had rejoiced that it was now 'GOD be thanked: a ruin!' with the 'peaceful Cross' planted in its centre (*PFI*). The Cross is all very well but the vividness of the imagery he uses to describe the sight of the Electric Telegraph in the ancient ruin suggests that this is something rejoices him even more (perhaps it was just as well that it wasn't Ruskin he was writing to).

The phrase about 'ages of darkness, wickedness, and violence' quoted in the preceding paragraph comes from *The Chimes* (1844) when poor old Trotty Veck has to undergo a series of harrowing visions, beginning with a severe reproof from the Goblin of the Great Bell for having believed Tory cant about 'the good old times' and even fancying he could hear the phrase echoed in the ringing of his beloved church chimes:

> 'The voice of Time,' said the Phantom [i. e., the Goblin], 'cries to man, Advance! Time IS for his advancement and improvement; for his greater worth, his greater happiness, his better life; his progress onward to that goal within its knowledge and its view, and set there in the period when Time and he began. Ages of darkness, wickedness, and violence, have come and gone: millions uncountable, have suffered, lived and died: to point the way Before him ... .
>
> 'Who puts into the mouth of Time, or of its servants ... a cry of lamentation for days which have had their trial and their failure, and have left deep traces of it which the

blind may see – a cry that only serves the Present Time, by showing men how much it needs their help when any ears can listen to regrets for such a Past – who does this, does a wrong. And you have done that wrong to us, the Chimes.'

The nature of the religious faith underpinning the belief in human progress expressed by Dickens in this passage will form the subject of my last chapter. I am quoting the passage here as one of the strongest expressions to be found in all his work (he was, he said, 'wrathful and red-hot' when he wrote this urgently topical second Christmas Book) of his progressive view of history.

For Dickens human history up to the 17th century seems to divide itself into two main epochs, rather like Thackeray's pre and post railway ones. First came the state of 'savagery' from which many races have not yet fully emerged, including Mrs Pardiggle's Tockahoopo Indians and Mrs Jellyby's Borrioboola-Ghaians 'on the left bank of the Niger' (*BH*, 4, 8). Thus, the first inhabitants of Britain were 'poor savages, going almost naked, or only dressed in the rough skins of beasts and staining their bodies, as other savages do, with coloured earths and the juices of plants', divided into tribes, each with 'its own little king' and 'constantly fighting with one another, as savage people usually do' (*CHE*). Few things enraged Dickens more than Romantic idealisation of the 'Noble Savage', a being gloriously 'unrestrained and unfettered' by civilisation, as George Catlin expressed it in his *Letters … on North American Indians* (1842). We have noted above (p. 24) Dickens's contempt for the Zulu warriors put on exhibition in London in 1853; after viewing them and recalling comparable earlier exhibitions of native Americans and Africans, Dickens indulged himself in a ferocious tirade:

> … I call a savage a something highly desirable to be civilised off the face of the earth. I think a mere gent

(which I take to be the lowest form of civilisation) better than a howling, whistling, clucking, stamping, jumping, tearing savage. It is all one to me, whether he sticks a fishbone through his visage, or bits of tree through the lobes of his ears, or birds' feathers in his hair .... Yielding to whichsoever of these agreeable eccentricities, he is a savage – cruel, false, thievish, murderous; addicted more or less to grease, entrails, and beastly customs .... (*HW*, 'The Noble Savage', 11 June 1853)

And in another piece about the 'lost Arctic voyagers' (the Franklin Expedition) he repeated his opinion, this time with respect to the Inuit people ('Esquimaux'): 'We believe every savage to be in his heart covetous, treacherous, and cruel' (*HW*, 2 Dec. 1854).

After the epoch of 'savagery' there followed for Europe (and presumably for North Africa and all of Asia, though Dickens shows scant interest in the history of those parts of the world – apart from occasional mockery of the petrified nature of Chinese civilisation) those 'ages of darkness, wickedness and violence' to which the Goblin of the Bell refers, providing ample evidence that covetousness, treachery and cruelty (our 'savage' heritage, referred to by Tennyson as 'the ape and tiger' in human nature that we must in time outgrow) by no means disappeared from the world with the beginnings of civilisation. The period of the decline and fall of the Roman Empire provides a particularly spectacular example of one of those dark and violent ages as Dickens's just-quoted response to the Colosseum indicates and as the startled Mr Boffin soon discovers ('I didn't think this morning there were so many Scarers in Print', he muses after his first day's exposure to the 'confounding enormities' related by Gibbon; *OMF*, 1. 5). As for Britain, its history from the Ancient Britons to the Stuarts as related by Dickens in his *Child's History of England* (serialised in *Household Words* 1851-1853) is chiefly a somewhat knockabout

catalogue of crimes, atrocities and acts of oppression committed by power-abusing kings and barons and priests (beginning
with the Druids and their penchant for burning people alive 'in
immense wicker cages'). Dickens, said Humphry House, 'used
the past ... as an additional field for his genius in describing the
unpleasant', adding with reference to Dickens's two historical
novels, 'the Gordon Riots and the French Revolution were
unpleasant on a panoramic scale'.

As regards the *Child's History*, Dickens seems to have
written a version of it eight years before publication for he told
Jerrold in a letter of 3 May 1843 that he is 'writing a little
history of England' to prevent his six-year-old son Charley
from getting hold 'of any conservative or High Church notions'
('the best way of guarding against any such horrible result,
is, I take it, to wring the parrots' necks in his very cradle').
Among the chief villains of Dickens's history are a prelate, the
Anglo-Saxon Abbot Dunstan ('an imperious, audacious, ill-
conditioned priest, who ... became a sour monk'), and a king,
Henry VIII, much approved of, we notice, by both Alderman
Cute in *The Chimes* ('stout King Hal, bluff King Hal. Ah. Fine
character!') and by the Hon. Mrs Skewton, who admires Hol-
bein's portrait of him in Warwick Castle 'with his dear little
peepy eyes, and his benevolent chin!' (*DS*, 27). For Dickens he
was simply 'a most intolerable ruffian, a disgrace to human
nature, and a blot of blood and grease upon the History of
England'. Heroes are much rarer in the *Child's History*, the one
attracting the highest praise being that 'good Saxon', King
Alfred, 'whose mighty heart never failed him' in his successful
battles against the plundering and marauding Danes, who
'never rested from his labours to improve his people', and 'who
loved justice, freedom, truth, and knowledge'. The praise of
Oliver Cromwell's vigorous rule ('it began to be thoroughly
well known, all over the world, that England was governed by
a man in earnest') no doubt owes something to Carlyle but
Dickens's extreme hostility towards the Stuarts ('a public nui-

sance altogether') is very much his own. He seems to have imagined the state of the country under James I ('His Sowship') or Charles II as peculiarly horrible – see, for example, his description of Will Marks's nocturnal entry into London in 'Mr Pickwick's Tale' (*MHC*). The tale is set in the reign of James I when, Dickens writes, 'none could walk the streets [of London] without danger of their lives' after nine in the evening 'and even at this hour robberies and murder were of no uncommon occurrence':

> There were kites and ravens feeding in the streets (the only scavengers the City kept) …. There were distant fires where the poor wood and plaster tenements wasted fiercely, and whither crowds made their way clamouring eagerly for plunder, beating down all who came within their reach, and yelling like devils let loose. There were single-handed men flying from bands of ruffians, who pursued them with naked weapons, and hunted them savagely; there were drunken desperates issuing from their dens and staggering through the open streets where no man dared molest them: there were vagabond servitors returning from the Bear Garden, where had been good sport that day, dragging after them their torn and bleeding dogs or leaving them to die and rot upon the road. Nothing was abroad but cruelty, violence and disorder.

To return briefly to the *Child's History*, Dickens ends that work with a reference to the 'great and glorious Revolution' of 1688 which established 'the Protestant religion' in England and, it is implied, ushered in a different age – Dickens's third 'epoch', as it were. This was the Eighteenth Century, the period in which both of his historical novels are set, and his attitude towards which we shall consider below.

The *Child's History* makes abundantly clear just what, in

Dickens's view, had always been, and still were, the greatest obstacles to progress of genuine civilisation in the history of Europe. One was autocratic rulers like the Tsars of Russia, a country Dickens refers to as being still in a 'barbaric' state (*LD*, II. 22). The other was the Roman Catholic Church, 'that curse upon the world', as he called it in a letter to Miss Coutts at the height of the 'Papal Aggression' hysteria of 1850, a hysteria to which Dickens himself energetically contributed through a rabidly satirical article, 'A Crisis in the Affairs of Mr John Bull' (*HW*, 23 Nov. 1850). The Catholic religion was one that, even 'in the dear old year one thousand seven hundred and seventy-five', countenanced in France the sentencing of a youth

> ... to have his hands cut off, his tongue torn out with pincers, and his body burned alive, because he had not kneeled down in the rain to do honour to a dirty procession of monks which passed within his view, at a distance of some fifty or sixty yards. (*TTC*, I. 1)

At the border between two Swiss cantons, one Protestant and the other Catholic, Dickens claimed that

> ... you might separate two perfectly distinct and different conditions of humanity by drawing a line with your stick in the dust on the ground. On the Protestant side, neatness; cheerfulness; industry; education; continual aspiration, at least, after better things. On the Catholic side, dirt, disease, squalor, and misery. (Forster, V. 3)

He had a set of dummy book backs made for his Tavistock House study in 1851 (they can still to be seen in situ at his last home, Gad's Hill Place) and among the spoof titles was a set called 'The Wisdom of Our Ancestors' with volumes entitled 'Ignorance', 'Superstition', 'The Block', 'The Stake', 'The Rack', 'Dirt', and 'Disease'. As this indicates, the insidious or violent suppression of individual freedom of thought or action, especially when directed towards the physical betterment of man's condition, like the battle against dirt and disease, was for Dickens, every inch a freeborn Protestant Englishman as he was, the greatest of all crimes against humanity, the greatest of all retardations of human progress. He rejoiced to live in what he called, in an 1851 speech proposing the health of Joseph Paxton, creator of the Crystal Palace,

> ... with all its faults ... a great age, when a man impressed with a useful idea, could carry out his project without being imprisoned, or thumb-screwed or persecuted in any form.

We have noted above Dickens's reactions to the prisons and the torture museum in Venice and there are comparable comments on the Palais des Papes at Avignon (in *PFI*) when he dwells, again with fascinated horror, on the activities of the Inquisition; also, when writing of Charles I's England he calls attention to the ear-cropping and nose-slitting activities of the authorities in their dealings with opponents of the Anglican establishment (*CHE*). The favoured Stuart doctrine of the Divine Right of Kings was absolute anathema to Dickens, of course, and we might recall here a passage in *Great Expectations* when he gleefully seizes an opportunity to mock it *en passant* (he is describing Pip's frowsty bedchamber at the Hummums in Covent Garden):

> ... a sort of vault on the ground floor at the back, with a despotic monster of a fourpost bedstead in it, straddling over the whole place, putting one of his arbitrary legs into the fireplace, and another into the doorway, and squeezing the wretched little washing-stand in quite a Divinely Righteous manner. (*GE*, 45)

It is true that Dickens endows Charles I with both nobility and pathos in his description in the *Child's History* of the King's last hours and execution (though his severed head had earlier been a running joke in *David Copperfield*, responding no doubt to the contemporary bicentenary commemoration of 'the Royal Martyr'). This sympathy with the condemned king, however, is like his sympathetic portrayal of Roman Catholics in *Barnaby Rudge*, or of the doomed French aristocrats awaiting the guillotine in *A Tale of Two Cities*; once individuals, no matter how repugnant the beliefs or values by which they have lived, become victims, or are on the verge of a violent death, Dickens at once begins to sympathise, or at least empathise, with them – even with the evil Fagin ('such an out-and-outer I don't know what to make of him', he wrote to Forster when finishing *Oliver Twist*) when the shadow of the gallows falls upon the old man. Fagin has also been hunted by the mob and in both his historical novels, Dickens makes it clear that he saw the mob as a worse tyrant even than priests and autocrats; he writes of it in *Barnaby Rudge* (ch. 52): 'the ocean is not more fickle and uncertain, more terrible when roused, more unreasonable, or more cruel'. Like Byron, Dickens wanted people to be free 'from mobs as well as kings; from you as well as me'.

As already noted, Dickens's historical novels are set in the 18th century and they contain figures that represent and express everything that he found most hateful in the culture of that age, an age for which he certainly had no Thackeray-style nostalgia and which he very much saw through Hogarthian spectacles (Dickens, Forster thought, 'closely resembled him [Hogarth] in genius'). Its aristocratic cultivation of style, wit and poise appeared to him essentially shallow and 'heartless' (we might compare here Matthew Arnold's notorious criticism that the poetry of Pope and Dryden was 'composed in the wits and not in the soul'); and all its highly polished and ultra-'civilised' behaviour co-existed with appalling social conditions of gross inequality, brutality (the exquisite beau 'whom it takes four men at once to shake into his buckskins ... goes to see all the executions' [*BH*, 12]), squalor and lawlessness:

> ... the Lord Mayor of London, was made to stand and deliver on Turnham Green, by one highwayman, who despoiled the illustrious creature in the sight of all his retinue; ... thieves snipped diamond crosses from the necks of noble lords at Court drawing-rooms ... the hangman, ever busy and ever worse than useless, was in constant requisition ... today taking the life of an atrocious murderer, and tomorrow of a wretched pilferer who had robbed a farmer's boy of sixpence. (*TTC*, I. 1)

The smoothly hypocritical and thoroughly villainous Mr (later Sir John) Chester in *Barnaby Rudge* is a caricature of the 18th century statesman and wit, the Earl of Chesterfield. He is presented as a devoted student of Chesterfield's *Letters to his Son*, a book that Dickens saw as the absolute epitome of 18th century worldliness. Mr Chester is at one point made to exclaim that the *Letters* contain 'the finest code of morality, and the most gentlemanly sentiments in the universe!':

> ... in every page of this enlightened writer, I find some captivating hypocrisy which never occurred to me before, or some superlative piece of selfishness to which I was utterly a stranger. I should quite blush for myself before this stupendous creature, if, remembering his precepts, one might blush at anything. (*BR*, ch. 23)

Nearly twenty years later Dickens gives us a sinister reprise of Mr Chester, not at all comic, in 'Monsieur the Marquis' in *A Tale of Two Cities*. With his perfect dress and manners, his 'fine mask' of a face, his utter callousness, and his brutal disdain for the common people, whom he treats as mere cattle, the Marquis represents, in Dickens's view, the culminating point of the culture of the *ancien régime* which had carried the 'heartless' aristocratic values of the 18th century to a much greater extreme than had the English ruling classes (unlike his real-life model, Mr Chester has no political power though he is cunning in manipulating the mob). The reason for this, Dickens would doubtless have argued, was that the power of kings, priests and aristocrats was much more circumscribed in England as a result of 1688, and partly also the 'English-Saxon' national character which Dickens, in an amazingly Podsnappian passage in the *Child's History*, claims to have shown itself to be 'the greatest character among the nations of the earth':

> Wheresoever that race goes, there, law, and industry, and safety for life and property, and all the great results of steady perseverance, are certain to arise

Even in the 18th-century England of *Barnaby Rudge* these virtues are shining with the honest locksmith Gabriel Varden and his daughter's lover, young Joe Willet as their chief representatives. Sturdy, plain-speaking, perennial English manliness confronts elegant, polished, 18th-century 'gentlemanliness' in the scene in Chapter 75 when Varden forces his way into Chester's bedchamber to plead with him to try to save Hugh, his unacknowledged natural son, from the gallows:

> '... Although you have, thrice within as many weeks, turned your lawful son, Mr Edward, from your door, you may have time, you may have years to make your peace with *him*, Sir John; but that twelve o'clock [when Hugh is to be hung] will soon be here, and soon be past for ever.'
>
> 'I thank you very much', returned the knight, kissing his delicate hand to the locksmith, 'for your guileless advice; and I only wish, my good soul, that you had a little more worldly wisdom. I never so much regretted the

arrival of my hair-dresser as I do at this moment. God bless you! Good morning! ...'

Unsurprisingly, given his strong belief in progress, social and moral as well as technological, Dickens was always roused to fiercely satirical wrath by any talk of 'the good old days', or any movement such as Disraeli's 'Young England' party in politics, or the Oxford Movement in the Church of England, or Pre-Raphaelitism in the world of art, that seemed to be looking back nostalgically to past times or even attempting to restore some aspects of them. He lampooned the Oxford Movement anonymously in *The Examiner* (3 June 1843; 'Report of the Commissioners Appointed to Inquire into the Condition of the Persons Variously Engaged in the University of Oxford'), attacked the Bishop of London for seeming to countenance it in 'A Crisis in the Affairs of Mr John Bull' (*HW*), and returned to the charge in *Bleak House* when describing the 'ladies and gentlemen' at Chesney Wold who 'would make the Vulgar very picturesque and faithful, by putting back the hands upon the Clock of Time, and cancelling a few hundred years of history'. Pre-Raphaelitism was closely linked to the Oxford Movement and was equally anathema to Dickens. His notorious denunciation of Millais's Pre-Raphaelite masterpiece, 'Christ in the House of His Parents', adopts a tone of angry sarcasm:

> There is something so fascinating ... in the notion of ignoring all that has been done for the happiness and elevation of mankind during three or four centuries of slow and dearly-bought amelioration, that we have always thought it would tend soundly to the improvement of the general public, if any tangible symbol ... expressive of that admirable conception, could be held up before them. We are happy to have found such a sign at last ... . ('Old Lamps for New Ones', *HW*, 15 June 1850)

Since the wonderful paintings produced by Raphael, Dickens writes, 'Beauty' has been considered one of the 'indispensable elements' of art but now here is a group of artists, dedicated to 'the great retrogressive principle', who propose to return to the aesthetics of the Middle Ages. This involves a kind of realism that Dickens evidently considers not only perversely retrograde but also little short of blasphemous when applied to Biblical subjects. Why not a Pre-Newtonian Brotherhood to deny the laws of gravitation or a Pre-Henry-the-Seventh Brotherhood to regulate social matters?

> This Society, as cancelling all the advances of nearly four hundred years, and reverting to one of the most disagreeable periods of English History, when the nation was yet very slowly emerging from barbarism ... must be regarded with peculiar favour. As the time of ugly religious caricatures (called mysteries), it is thoroughly Pre-Raphael in its spirit ... . We should be certain of the Plague among other advantages, if this Brotherhood were properly encouraged.

Just as obnoxious to Dickens as those who want to put the clock back are those who simply stop it like Mr Turveydrop, the 'Model of Deportment' in *Bleak House*, who continues to live the life of a Regency dandy (grossly exploiting his devoted son in order to do so), or that other group of ladies and gentlemen at Chesney Wold who seem determined to perpetuate the Chesterfieldian culture of the 18th century:

> For whom everything must be languid and pretty. Who have found out the perpetual stoppage. Who are to rejoice at nothing, and be sorry for nothing. Who are not to be disturbed by ideas. On whom even the Fine Arts, attending in powder and walking backward like the Lord Chamberlain, must array themselves in the milliners' and

tailors' patterns of past generations, and be particularly careful not to be in earnest, or to receive any impress from the moving age. (*BH*, 12)

'The moving age.' This phrase succinctly expresses Dickens's dynamic conception of the age in which he lived, one in which such massive strides were being made in social improvement — with the help of advancing science and technology. There could be no tolerance of lingering relics of 'the good old days' such as criminal neighbourhoods that the police said were no-go areas:

> To tell us in open court ... that a costly police-system such as was never before this heard of, has left in London, in the days of steam and gas and photographs of thieves and electric telegraphs, the sanctuaries and stews of the Stuarts! Why, a parity of practice, in all departments, would bring back the Plague in two summers, and the Druids in a century. (*UT*, 'On an Amateur Beat'; *ATYR*, 27 Feb. 1869)

Aside from the cleaning up of such retrograde relics of the 'bad old days' (the Court of Chancery, 'most pestilent of hoary sinners', being, of course, one of the very worst), there was an immense amount for 'the moving age' to strive for. There was a world of things to be done, for example, with regard to such basic requisites for social progress as public education and sanitary reform. Alongside the display of the world's 'peaceful glories' in the Crystal Palace there should be, suggested Dickens in his 'Last Words of the Old Year' (*HW*, 4 Jan. 1851), 'another Exhibition — for a great display of England's sins and negligences, to be, by steady contemplation of all eyes, and steady union of all hearts and hands, set right'.

We notice here that Dickens talks of a 'steady union of all hearts and hands' rather than of Parliamentary legislation, and

we have noted in the previous chapter his general contempt for
M.P.s and their Parliamentary activities. Whatever other signs
of 'hopeful' progress Dickens observed in the contemporary
scene, developments in the nation's political institutions were
not among them. What, he might have asked, had been the
results of the greatest political event of his young manhood, the
passing of the 1832 Reform Bill (the progress of which through
Parliament he had, as a young reporter, witnessed at close
quarters)? Its supporters maintained that it would bring in a
better, juster era as a result of a more equal distribution of the
franchise, the abolition of 'rotten boroughs', and so on. But one
of the chief works of the Reformed House of Commons was the
New Poor Law, loathed by Dickens as inhumane, unjust and
retrogressive in spirit, yet still working its mischief when he
wrote the Postscript to *Our Mutual Friend* thirty years later,
declaring:

I believe there has been in England, since the days of the
STUARTS, no law so often infamously administered, no
law so openly violated, no law habitually so ill-super-
vised.

And alongside the harshness of the new Utilitarianism that
created such a Poor Law old electoral abuses still continued, as
the young journalist saw at first hand, when reporting a by-
election at Kettering in 1835. He wrote for *The Morning Chronicle* (19 Dec. 1835):

No artifice has been left untried, no influence has been
withheld, no chicanery neglected by the Tory party; and
the glorious result is, that Mr Maunsell is placed at the
head of the poll, by the most ignorant, drunken, and
brutal electors in these kingdoms, who have been treated
and fed, and driven up to the polls the whole day, like
herds of swine.

Throughout his fiction, from the riotous Eatanswill election in *Pickwick* through the election in *Bleak House* (40) when Lord Doodle finds it necessary to 'throw himself upon the country – chiefly in the form of sovereigns and beer' – to the phoney electioneering of Podsnap, Lady Tippins and their cronies in *Our Mutual Friend* as they 'work' to 'bring in' their friend Veneering for the constituency of Pocket-Breaches, Dickens presents a uniformly satirical picture of the workings of 19th century democracy. The Crimean War crisis and all the Parliamentary manoeuvrings it led to exasperated him and his like-minded friends to the highest pitch. 'The people of England', wrote Walter Savage Landor, Dickens's model for Boythorn in *Bleak House*, in *The Atlas* (22 Sept. 1855),

> ... stand on one side; on the other 500 Whigs and Tories in two assembly-rooms (one above stairs, the other below), dancing until they are dizzy, and shuffling and cutting, and capering and crossing hands ....

To Dickens there seemed to be no hope of real political progress until after there had been enormous progress in the field of public education and some abatement of foolish aristocracy-worship. 'As to the suffrage,' he wrote to Macready on 4 October 1855:

> I have lost hope even in the Ballot [as a means of achieving more honest elections]. We appear to me to have proved the failure of Representative Institutions, without an educated and advanced people to support them. What with teaching people to 'keep in their stations' ... what with having no such thing as a Middle Class (for, though we are perpetually boasting of it as our safety, it is nothing but a poor fringe on the mantle of the Upper) – what with flunkeyism, toadyism, letting the most contemptible Lords come in for all manner of places –

making asses of ourselves for Prince Albert to saddle – reading the Court Circular for the New Testament ... I do reluctantly believe that the English people are, habitually, consenting parties to the miserable imbecility into which we have fallen, and never will help themselves out of it ... .

Twelve years later he saw the Second Reform Bill, which widened the franchise to include a substantial section of the working classes, the famous 'ten-pound householders', as the inevitable, and deplorable, result of putting the electoral cart before the educational horse:

... it should have been, and could have been, perfectly known to any honest man in England that the more intelligent part of the great masses were deeply dissatisfied with the present state of representation, but were in a very moderate and patient condition, awaiting the better intellectual cultivation of numbers of their fellows. The old insolent resource of assailing them and making the most audaciously wicked statements that they are politically indifferent, has borne the inevitable fruit. The perpetual taunt, 'Where are they?' has called them out with the answer: 'Well, then, if you must know, here we are'. The intolerable injustice of vituperating the bribed to an assembly of bribers, has goaded their sense of injustice beyond endurance. And now, what they would have taken they won't take, and whatever they are steadily bent upon having they will get ... .

(letter to William de Cerjat, 1 Jan. 1867)

He adds that he does not share apprehensions about the possible result of power passing into the hands of the working classes:

> I have such a very small opinion of what the great genteel
> have done for us, that I am very philosophical indeed
> concerning what the great vulgar may do, having a de-
> cided opinion that they can't do worse.

Whatever the age's achievements in science, technology,
industry and improved social conditions, then, it was certainly
not for Dickens an age of political progress — indeed, one rather
forms the impression that he did not believe any significant
advance in the organisation of the nation's political life had
occurred since 1688. Nor had he, as the passages just quoted
show, much faith in political movements aimed at reforming or
enhancing the workings of Parliamentary democracy so long as
public education remained so neglected. The major Parliamentary reform movement in his time was Chartism, Dickens's
attitude towards which can be deduced from the words he puts
into the mouth of 'Old John', the Birmingham workman and
inventor who tells 'A Poor Man's Tale of a Patent' (*HW*, 19
Oct. 1850):

> I am not a Chartist, and I never was. I don't mean to say
> but what I see a good many public points to complain of,
> still I don't think that's the way to set them right. If I did
> think so, I should be a Chartist. But I don't think so, and
> I am not a Chartist. I read the paper, and hear discussion,
> at what we call 'a parlor' in Birmingham, and I know
> many good men and workmen who are Chartists. Note.
> Not Physical force.

Dickens shared to the full middle-class fears of the 'Physical
Force' Chartists who wanted to achieve their aims through
violence, and gives a nightmare glimpse of them in *The Old
Curiosity Shop* (1840-41) when Nell and her Grandfather are
fleeing through the 'blackened' industrial town (45):

... bands of unemployed labourers ... clustered by torchlight round their leaders, who told them, in stern language, of their wrongs, and urged them on to frightful cries and threats; when maddened men, armed with sword and firebrand ... rushed forth on errands of terror and destruction, to work no ruin half so surely as their own.

He has somewhat modified the tone of high melodrama by the time he comes, fourteen years later, to describe the inflammatory harangues of the agitator Slackbridge to the Coketown 'hands' (*HT*, II. 4) but the underlying belief is the same, that an uneducated or semi-educated populace is liable always to fall victim to corrupt manipulation of one kind or another – which seems somewhat to contradict his famous statement of his 'political creed' in a speech at a meeting of the Birmingham and Midland Institute the year before he died. His political beliefs were, he said,

... contained in two articles, and [had] no reference to any party or persons. My faith in the people governing is, on the whole, infinitesimal; my faith in The People governed, is, on the whole, illimitable. [*Loud applause*]

He would have represented his position more precisely if he had added after 'illimitable' the words 'but they need to be given access to education'.

Before leaving the topic of Dickens and Progress a point should be noted that will surely strike anyone who begins to read extensively in his fiction and that is the contrast between his passionate (if not exactly 'steam-whistle') enthusiasm for new developments in technology, or for reforms (educational, sanitary, legal) that will help to bring about a fairer, more humane, and more tolerant society, and that element in his work that House calls 'the urge back to the past'. House was pointing to the fact that much of Dickens's fiction is set, wholly or partially, not in the contemporary world but in the richly-evoked world of his childhood and early youth as in the case of *Pickwick Papers*, *Nicholas Nickleby*, *The Old Curiosity Shop*, *Martin Chuzzlewit* (which features in chapter 36 a vivid evocation of the joys of stage-coach travel in England; the American scenes, on the other hand, are very definitely contemporary), *David Copperfield*, certain elements in *Bleak House*, much of *Little Dorrit* (though the Circumlocution Office satire and the Merdle mania are very much of the 1850s); and *Great Expectations*.

This repeated mining of the seemingly inexhaustible seam of his memories of those early years follows naturally from the fact that it was the impressions and experiences of those years that affected him most profoundly, that formed and so richly nourished the world of his imagination, together with his early reading as already noted (*The Arabian Nights*, *Pilgrim's Progress*, *Robinson Crusoe* and so on) and early experience of theatre. Above all, Forster tells us, it was during his happy childhood years in Chatham that 'the most durable of his early impressions were received; and the associations that were around him when he died, were those which at the outset of his life had affected him most strongly.' Also very strong in their effect on him were the immediately succeeding experiences of his boyhood – as a desolated little 'labouring hind' in London, as a pupil at Wellington House Academy, and as a young lawyer's clerk. In a wonderful New Year's Day essay, 'Where We Stopped Growing' (*HW*, 1 Jan. 1853), Dickens recalls, in astonishingly vivid detail, first some of the literature and then some of the real things (objects, places, odd characters seen in the street) that fired his childish imagination, and the impression of which remained as fresh upon him as it had been then; he had never 'outgrown' them:

There was a poor demented woman who used to roam about the City, dressed all in black with cheeks staringly painted, and thence popularly known as Rouge et Noir; whom we have never outgrown by the height of a grain of mustard seed. The story went that her only brother, a Bank-clerk, was left for death for forgery; and that she, broken-hearted creature, lost her wits on the morning of his execution, and ever afterwards, while her confused dream of life lasted, flitted thus among the busy money-changers. A story, alas! all likely enough; but, likely or unlikely, true or untrue, never to take other shape in our mind ....

Another very different person who stopped our growth, we associate with Berners Street, Oxford Street ... . The White Woman is her name. She is dressed entirely in white, with a ghastly white plaiting round her head and face, inside her white bonnet. She even carries (we hope) a white umbrella. With white boots we know she picks her way through the winter dirt. She is a conceited old creature ... and evidently went simpering mad on personal grounds alone – no doubt because a wealthy Quaker wouldn't marry her. This is her bridal dress ... .

The probable connection (first examined by Harry Stone) between these two figures, seen by Dickens as a child and never 'outgrown' by him, and his much later creation of the haunting figure of Miss Havisham is one striking example of the artistic result of that constant mining of his earliest experiences referred to above.

Dickens did not outgrow such childhood experiences and nor, as is abundantly clear from *David Copperfield*, did he outgrow his immediately following experiences as a young reporter first in Doctors' Commons and then in Parliament (we have noted above the rowdy, corrupt by-election he covered in 1835 which must certainly have contributed to the creation of Eatanswill in Pickwick) and as the devoted, tormented lover of

Maria Beadnell, to whom, as Mrs Winter, he wrote many years later:

> Whatever of fancy, romance, energy, passion, aspiration
> and determination belong to me, I have never separated
> and never shall separate from the hard-hearted little
> woman — you — whom it is nothing to say I would have
> died for, with the greatest alacrity! (15 Feb. 1855)

Small wonder, then, that he should return so often in his fiction to the world of his childhood, youth and early manhood. But, even when he may sound nostalgic about the past as, for example, in his great Uncommercial Traveller essay, 'Dullborough Town' (1860), when he describes returning to 'Dullborough' (i. e., Rochester), the scene of his happy childhood and the 'birthplace of his fancy', it is rather a question of yearning for an (inevitably) lost personal world of 'innocent fancy' than of any general elegiac lament for past 'good old days', such as George Eliot's threnody for the days of 'Fine old Leisure' in *Adam Bede* (52), or Thackeray's for the lost world of his younger days in his 'De Juventute' ('They have raised those railroad embankments up, and shut off the old world that was behind them. Climb up that bank on which the irons are laid, and look to the other side — it is gone').

Dickens's view of the *public* world of the early 19th century, the world into which he was born and in which he grew up, was anything but nostalgic. 'The fine old English Tory times', he called them in a Radical squib he wrote for *The Examiner* in 1841, when the Tories had been returned to power under Peel. It was a parody of 'The Fine Old English Gentleman', a new version 'to be said or sung at all Conservative dinners' and it seems appropriate to end this chapter by quoting one or two of the verses:

In those rare days, the press was seldom known to snarl or
    bark,
But sweetly sang of men in pow'r, like any tuneful lark;
Grave judges, too, to all their evil deeds were in the dark;
And not a man in twenty score knew how to make his mark.
    Oh the fine old English Tory times;
    Soon may they come again!

Those were the days for taxes; and for war's infernal din;
For scarcity of bread, that fine old dowagers might win;
For shutting men of letters up, through iron bars to grin,
    Because they didn't think the Prince was altogether thin
    In the fine old English Tory times;
    Soon may they come again!

              ✦

The bright old day now dawns again; the cry runs through the
    land,
In England there shall be dear bread — In Ireland, sword and
    brand;
And poverty and ignorance, shall swell the rich and grand,
So, rally round the rulers with the gentle iron hand
    Of the fine old English Tory days;
    Hail to the coming time!

Home

Before marriage and afterwards, let [young couples] learn to centre all their hopes of real and lasting happiness in their own fireside; let them cherish the faith that in home, and all the English virtues which the love of home engenders, lies the only true source of domestic felicity; let them believe that round the household gods, contentment and tranquillity cluster in their gentlest and most graceful forms; and that many weary hunters of happiness through the noisy world, have learned this truth too late, and found a cheerful spirit and a quiet mind only at home at last.

'Conclusion' to *Sketches of
Young Couples* (1840)

No man was so inclined naturally to derive his happiness from home concerns. Even the kind of interest in a house which is commonly confined to women, he was full of. Not to speak of changes of importance, there was not an additional hook put up wherever he inhabited, without his knowledge, or otherwise than as part of some small ingenuity of his own.

(Forster, XI. 3)

One of the best-known scenes in all Dickens's work is the Cratchits' Christmas dinner in the *Carol*. In their little four-roomed house in Camden Town the joyfully-reunited family feast on a roast goose, the youngest Cratchits being 'steeped in sage and onions to the eyebrows', and a Christmas pudding of modest dimensions 'blazing in half-a-quartern of ignited brandy'. After the meal they all draw round the hearth, 'in what Bob Cratchit called a circle, meaning half a one', for the post-prandial delights of roasted chestnuts and toasts drunk in steaming punch ('"God bless us every one!" said Tiny Tim'). The episode is Dickens's most memorable celebration of those 'home affections' that he profoundly believed to be so hugely important not only for the moral health and spiritual welfare of individuals but, as we shall see, very important also, especially as manifested among the poorer classes, for the very stability of the nation as a whole.

Christmas is, of course, the great family festival (first celebrated as such by Dickens in an early sketch, 'Christmas Festivities', originally published in *Bell's Life in London* on 27 December 1835 and reprinted in *Sketches by Boz* with the more focused title of 'A Christmas Dinner'). It is not, therefore, surprising that it is in his series of little books written for the Christmas market (1843-48), of which the *Carol* was the glorious prototype, that we find such frequent and intense insistence on the joys and rewards of domesticity. The third of these 'Christmas Books', *The Cricket on the Hearth*, is indeed subtitled 'A Fairy Tale of Home', and begins with several pages of rhapsodic writing about a boiling kettle and a chirping cricket combining to produce a 'fireside song of comfort' to welcome home the carter John Peerybingle. It celebrates his return, after the day's work in the rain and the cold, to his humble cottage and his much younger, pretty little 'dumpling' of a wife and their little baby (John Leech's delightful illustration of the scene shows a whole choir of putti spiralling upwards in the steam of the kettle). Later, Peerybingle thinks he has reason to suspect his wife of infidelity but is rebuked by the Cricket, who appears to him 'in Fairy shape' upon the hearth by which he sits brooding darkly:

'The hearth she has – how often! – blessed and bright-ened,' said the Cricket; 'the hearth which, but for her, were only a few stones and bricks and rusty bars, but which has been through her, the Altar of your Home; on which you have nightly sacrificed some petty passion, selfishness, or care, and offered up the homage of a tranquil mind, a trusting nature, and an overflowing heart; so that the smoke from this poor chimney has gone upward with a better fragrance than the richest incense that is burnt before the richest shrines in all the gaudy temples of this world! – Upon your own hearth; in its quiet sanctuary; surrounded by its gentle influences and associations; hear her! Hear me! Hear everything that speaks the language of your hearth and home!'

This (no doubt part of the 'petit-bourgeois sentimentality' that drove Lenin from the theatre when he attended a stage version of the story in Moscow in 1922) is one of Dickens's fullest and most direct expressions of his deeply-held lifelong belief in the sacred nature of Home, which, as Alexander Welsh persuasively argued in his *City of Dickens*, seems to have represented for him the Heavenly City brought down to earth. In each of the Christmas Books appears an apostate central character who has to be redeemed from misanthropy, distrust, cynicism or bitterness, and restored, like John Peerybingle, to belief and active participation in domestic joys and happiness. Scrooge is the great prototype, of course. He sullenly excludes himself from his nephew's Christmas family circle and his 'small fire in the grate' and 'little saucepan of gruel' consumed in solitude are the very antitheses of the cheerful hearth with its brightly-shining fire and the tasty, lovingly-shared meal that are always for Dickens the great emblems of Home. But after his conversion Scrooge does go to his nephew's and finds himself 'at home in five minutes' and he also becomes 'a second father' to Tiny Tim. 'What's home?' exclaims the curmudgeonly Tackleton in the *Cricket*, 'Four walls and a ceiling!'; and the misguided Dr. Jeddler echoes him in *The Battle of Life*: 'a real home is only four walls; and a fictitious one, mere rags and ink'. Both characters have very different sentiments by the end of the stories in which they appear. Not one but *two* happy families, as well as one engaged couple, are clustered around the redeemed Redlaw for a joyous Christmas feast at the end of *The Haunted Man* (this volume, the last in the series, also contains another vividly-realised poor but happy and loving family, the Tetterbys, who are fully worthy of comparison with the Cratchits).

The Christmas Books certainly confirmed Dickens in the eyes of his vast and devoted readership as quintessentially the great novelist of domesticity, the grand exponent of English 'fireside happiness'. Reviewing *The Battle of Life* on Christmas Eve 1846, Dickens's old newspaper *The Morning Chronicle* said:

If this climate of ours had only been sunny and dry, instead of cold and rainy, we very much doubt whether Mr Dickens would have enjoyed the high position in literature which he now enjoys. He is so peculiarly a writer of home life, a delineator of household gods, and a painter of domestic scenes, that we feel convinced, had Italy, or Spain, or any country nearer the tropics than ours produced him, instead of describing lazzaroni, and maccaroni, and water melons, or Andalusian young ladies, and cigaritos, and chocolate, and mantillas, he would have migrated to our more northern shores for the sake of firesides, purring cats, boiling kettles, Dutch clocks and chirping crickets.

This reviewer, though evidently referring primarily to *The Cricket on the Hearth*, was doubtless remembering also various scenes of domestic happiness and contentment from Dickens's earlier fiction, such as the Nicklebys with 'all the peace and cheerfulness of home' restored to them in the little cottage at Bow (*NN*, 35), the Nubbles family, or the Garlands, in *The Old Curiosity Shop* (10, 38), or the 'triangular parlour and two small bedrooms' that form such a domestic heaven for those two favourites of their creator, Tom Pinch and his sister Ruth in *Martin Chuzzlewit* (39). From *Dombey and Son* onwards, however, the Home is a rather more precarious institution in Dickens's fiction and his stories tend to revolve around houses, often impressive family mansions, that are very much *not* homes, like Dombey's 'house of dismal state' near Portman Square, the Dedlocks' Chesney Wold (*BH*), Gradgrind's Stone Lodge (*HT*), the grandiose 'Merdle establishment in Harley Street, Cavendish Square' (*LD*, 21) where Mrs Merdle reposes on her 'nest of crimson and gold cushions', and the dark and dingy old City house to which Arthur Clennam so despondingly returns at the beginning of *Little Dorrit*, in a chapter with the ironic title 'Home' – one might add Miss Havisham's Satis House here also, and the Veneerings' 'bran-new house in a bran-new quarter of London' (*OMF*). Although Dickens does still paint a glowing domestic vignette from time to time, e. g. the Toodles' cosy home in *Dombey*, or the Bagnets' in *Bleak House*, or the Crisparkles' in *Drood*, happy homes are mostly, as far as the central characters are concerned, only to be seen, painfully, from the outside. Florence Dombey, unable to approach her own father, cannot stop watching a series of happy domestic tableaux in a real home across the street where there is an obvious strong bond between the widowed father and his eldest child, a little daughter who, when he returns home in the evening,

> … made his tea for him – happy little housekeeper she was then! and sat conversing with him … until the candles came. He made her his companion … (*DS*, 18)

Childless (as she supposes) Lady Dedlock, in the dreary grandeur of Chesney Wold, looks out

> ... in the early twilight from her boudoir at a keeper's lodge, and seeing the light of a fire upon the latticed panes, and smoke rising from the chimney, and a child, chased by a woman, running out into the rain to meet the shining figure of a wrapped up man coming through the gate, [is] quite put out of temper. (*BH*, 2)

*

In these novels Dickens seems to be more concerned with domesticity frustrated, or with the destruction or subversion of domestic havens and the ideal of Home, either by outside enemies or by failure within the walls. *David Copperfield* is full of such wrecked or failed homes, for example, and, in *Dombey* it is only thanks to the steadfast heroism of Captain Cuttle that the Little Wooden Midshipman manages to survive its 'going to pieces' so that it may yet become a temporary home for Florence (who, by the neat and skilful way in which she fills the Captain's pipe for him shows herself to be as natural a 'home-maker' as Dot Peerybingle herself, and Dot was, writes Dickens in the *Cricket*, 'out and out, the very best filler of a pipe, I should say, in the four quarters of the globe'. Even Mr Jarndyce's *Bleak House* cannot safeguard all its inhabitants from suffering and death, and all Little Dorrit's moving efforts to make a true Home out of her father's prison-cell and to exert a benificent 'Home' influence on him and on her siblings are subverted by the moral rot that the prison has produced in all of them but herself. In *A Tale of Two Cities* it is not his loving family circle but the hopeless love of another man for his wife that saves Darnay from the guillotine, and in *Great Expectations* Mrs Joe's tyrannical temper, she being, as Joe puts it, 'somewhat given to government', makes home a very uncomfortable place both for Joe and for the little brother she is 'bringing up by hand'. One of the last homes Dickens ever described is humble indeed but also hideous:

> Mother had the gripe and clutch of Poverty upon her face, upon her figure, and not least of all upon her voice. Her sharp and high-pitched words were squeezed out of her, as by the compression of bony fingers on a leather bag, and she had a way of rolling her eyes about and about the cellar, as she scolded, that was gaunt and hungry. Father, with his shoulders rounded, would sit quiet on a three-legged stool, looking at the empty grate, until she would pluck the stool from under him, and bid him go bring some money home. Then he would dismally ascend the steps, and I, holding my ragged shirt and trousers together with a hand (my only braces), would feint and dodge from Mother's pursuing grasp at my hair. (*GSE*)

All this emphasis on failed or unsatisfactory homes does not, of course, mean that Dickens has lost faith in his ideal – quite the opposite, in fact. No doubt it relates primarily to the fact that unhappy families provide novelists, as Tolstoy suggests at the beginning of *Anna Karenina*, with better story-lines than do happy ones, but it also seems most likely that the more Dickens's own domestic situation came under strain, culminating in the marital break-down of 1858, the more passionately he clung to the ideal but now with a much keener sense of its elusiveness and precariousness. In his last completed novel he is certainly intending us to feel as disturbed as Mortimer Lightwood does when Mortimer's dilettante friend Eugene makes fun of 'the domestic virtues'. Eugene has had a neat little kitchen fitted up in the chambers he shares with Mortimer and mockingly suggests that 'the domestic virtues' may assert themselves simply as a result of the proximity of so many kitchen implements:

'See!' said Eugene, 'miniature flour-barrel, rolling-pin, spice-box, shelf of brown jars, chopping-board, coffee-mill, dresser elegantly furnished with crockery, saucepans and pans, roasting jack, a charming kettle, an armoury of dish-covers. The moral influence of these objects, in forming the domestic virtues, may have an immense influence upon me ...' (*OMF*, II. 6)

And it is in this novel also that Dickens returns very strongly to the theme of the happy, modest home when he portrays the married life of Mr and Mrs John Rokesmith, whose kitchen is certainly not just there as a joke about domesticity:

But, John gone to business and Bella returned home, the dress would be laid aside, trim little wrappers and aprons would be substituted, and Bella ... would enter on the household affairs of the day. Such weighing and mixing and chopping and grating, such dusting and washing and polishing, such snipping and weeding and trowelling and other small gardening, such making and mending and folding and airing .... (*OMF*, IV. 5)

To invoke Mrs Peerybingle again, even she, we feel, 'blithe, thriving, steady little Dot' as she is, can hardly compete with this amount of purposeful domestic bustle.

Obviously, Dickens was, in his idealisation of 'hearth and home' and the family circle, very much a man of his age, an age when the British monarchy under Victoria and Albert was reconstituted as a highly domestic institution, when so much was written about the moral and spiritual power that could and should flow from the home and the family, when even so wild and strange a story of dysfunctional families and domestic violence as *Wuthering Heights* ends with the establishment of the idyllic domesticity of Hareton and the young Catherine, when the 'domestic drama' became the dominant genre in popular theatre (Jerrold claimed to have inaugurated it all with his highly successful *The Rent Day* at Drury Lane in 1832, a play in which, as his son Blanchard expressed it, 'the interest is fireside throughout'), when domestic subjects and genre scenes were so much favoured by painters. The cultural and social-historical reasons for all this have been much explored as, for example, by Walter Houghton in his seminal work *The Victorian Frame of Mind 1830-1870* (1957) and space forbids any examination of them here. It is, however, worth just noting how, through the very nature of his books, Dickens was in himself a remarkable intensifier of the cult of domesticity. Walter Bagehot, writing in *The National Review* in 1858 about the Cheap Edition of the novelist's works, noted:

> The penetrating power of this remarkable genius among all classes at home is not inferior to its diffusive energy abroad. The phrase 'household book' has, when applied to the works of Mr Dickens, a peculiar propriety. There is no contemporary English writer, whose works are read so generally throughout the whole house, who can give pleasure to the servants as well as the mistress, to the children as well as to the master.

It was in full awareness of this unique status of his that Dickens wrote excitedly to Forster in 1845 about an idea he had for establishing a cheap new weekly periodical:

> *Carol* philosophy, cheerful views, sharp anatomisation of humbug, jolly good temper; papers always in season, pat to the time of year; and a vein of glowing, hearty, generous, mirthful, beaming reference in everything to Home and Fireside. And I would call it, sir, –

THE CRICKET.
A cheerful creature that chirrups on the Hearth.
Natural History.

... I would come out, sir, with a prospectus on the subject of the Cricket that should put everybody in a good temper, and make such a dash at people's fenders and arm-chairs as hasn't been made for many a long day .... I would at once sit down upon their very hobs ....
(Forster, V. 1)

Writing this, Dickens already knew very well that he had a unique ascendancy over all the fenders, arm-chairs and hobs in thousands of homes throughout the country. 'There is not a fireside in the kingdom', wrote a reviewer of *David Copperfield* in *Fraser's Magazine* (Dec. 1850), 'where the cunning fellow has not contrived to secure a corner for himself as one of the dearest, and, by this time, one of the oldest friends of the family' (Trollope, writing his obituary of Dickens, surely found the perfect simile to express the phenomenal nature of the sales of his books; Dickens's novels, he said, must surely be consumed in families 'like legs of mutton or loaves of bread'). It was inevitable that when Dickens did in 1850 finally succeed in establishing his weekly journal, *Household Words*, he should quickly plump for a title that still implied a 'dash' at domestic firesides ('The Household Voice', 'The Household Guest', and 'The Household Face' were among other titles he considered before happily hitting upon so apt a quotation from Shakespeare's *Henry V*: 'Familiar in their mouths as household words').

In the little Christmas Book that was, in the event, the result of his 'Cricket' notion Dickens applies the phrase 'quiet sanctuary' to the Peerybingle home and he certainly would have largely agreed with the following much-quoted definition by Ruskin in his *Sesame and Lilies* (1865):

This is the true nature of home — it is the place of Peace; the shelter, not only from all injury, but from all terror, doubt and confusion. In so far as it is not this, it is not

home; so far as the anxieties of the outer life penetrate
into it, and the inconsistently-minded, unknown, un-
loved, or hostile society of the outer world is allowed by
either husband or wife to cross the threshold, it ceases to
be home; it is then only a part of the outer world which
you have roofed over, and lighted fire in … .

In the dominant ideology of early and mid-Victorian Britain
it was woman's nature and her destiny to be the guardian and
presiding genius of the Home, 'a cheerful female eidolon' in
Alexander Welsh's phrase, and, even if a home had no walls or
roof and nothing but 'the glow-worm in the cold grass' for its
only fire, a 'true wife', says Ruskin, could still ensure its
existence: 'Wherever [she] comes, this home is always round
her'. A splendidly Dickensian version of Ruskin's wife who
may find herself houseless but who still remains a home-creator
is the perfect soldier's wife, Mrs Bagnet in *Bleak House*, who
has had, perforce, to lead an itinerant life and who has been
beheld washing greens for her family's meals everywhere 'except upon a baggage waggon'. But, like other admirable wives
in Dickens's novels and in many of his contemporaries', she
differs from the purdah-like Ruskinian ideal in that the cares
and anxieties of the outer world are not kept from penetrating
to the Bagnet hearth; they do so in the form of the trouble that
falls upon her husband's beloved friend and comrade, Mr
George, and, far from withdrawing into some domestic sanc-
tum, Mrs Bagnet can and does sally forth into that outer world
to seek the means to resolve them.

The prototype for Dickens's more conventional Angel in the
House (or rather, Angel-in-waiting when we see her initially)
is Rose Maylie in *Oliver Twist*. At first sight she might seem
altogether ethereal but

… the changing expression of sweetness and good humour,
the thousand lights that played about the face, and left no

shadow there; above all, the smile, the cheerful, happy smile, were made for Home, and fireside peace and happiness. (*OT*, 39)

In the light of this description, it seems, on the face of it, somewhat surprising that Dickens objected so strongly to the so-called 'Fireside Plate', Cruikshank's last illustration for *Oliver Twist*, which shows Rose very much as the focal point of a fireside family group with Oliver at her knee, and her husband and mother by adoption comfortably with her seated around the domestic hearth. The problem was, apparently, that, as Forster pointed out to the publisher, the scene too closely resembled a well-known advertisement for hair-oil. Dickens would surely have been highly sensitive to any reduction to visual cliché of his glowing vision of the domestic bliss in which, after all his sufferings in the cruel and treacherous outer world, Oliver is lapped at the end of the novel.

Rose the home-angel has many successors in Dickens's work, some only just glimpsed in passing like the little girl in 'What Christmas Is As We Grow Older' (*CS*; *HW* Extra Christmas Number for 1851) on whose 'quiet and contented little face, we see Home fairly written', and they have been much discussed, usually with some hostility (George Orwell famously described *David Copperfield*'s Agnes as 'the most disagreeable of [Dickens's] heroines, the real legless angel of Victorian romance'). It is enough for our purposes here simply to note the prominence and persistence of the type in Dickens as fundamental to his concept of Home.

Any movement directed towards giving women a greater role, or indeed any role at all, outside the home was regarded by most Victorian opinion-formers as a major threat to their continuing to function in their 'natural' role as home-makers. The strength of the fear that talk about 'Women's Rights' inspired in the dominant patriarchal culture of the day can be judged by the over-the-top public reaction to the campaign for women's dress reform, known as 'Bloomerism', when it was imported into Britain from America in the autumn of 1851. The dress invented by Amelia Bloomer was based on Turkish female costume with loose trousers gathered at the ankle and worn beneath a knee-length skirt. It gave women much greater freedom of literal movement, and was closely associated with the whole issue of 'Women's Rights'. *Punch* was crammed with cartoons and paragraphs obsessively ridiculing the 'Bloomers' and clearly revealing the profound anxiety about 'gender-bending', as we now call it, that was evidently at the heart of this virulent hostility ('Sweet love', Tennyson had warned a few years earlier in *The Princess*, would be 'slain' if women were to become at all masculinised). Dickens joined in in *Household Words* (8 Nov. 1851) with an article entitled 'Sucking Pigs' (referring back to an earlier one called 'Whole Hogs' that attacked fanatics of various kinds). He expresses serio-comic horror about women like the 'Bloomers' who campaigned in public (a 'London Bloomer Committee' had been formed, and public meetings were being addressed by both American and British female lecturers) and, assuming the persona of an anxious husband, writes:

> ... we admit that our mind would be disturbed, if our own domestic well-spring were to consider it necessary to entrench herself behind a small table ornamented with a water bottle and tumbler, and from that fortified position to hold forth to the public. Similarly, we should doubt the expediency of her putting up for Marylebone, or being one of the Board of Guardians for St Pancras, or serving on the Grand Jury for Middlesex ... [etc., etc.].

He clearly saw the 'sanctuary' aspect of Home as threatened, if not altogether destroyed, when women took to public life:

> ... should we love our Julia better, if she were a Member

of Parliament, a Parochial Guardian, a High Sheriff, a Grand Juror, or a woman distinguished for her able conduct in the chair? Do we not, on the contrary, rather seek in the society of our Julia, a haven of refuge from members of Parliament, Parochial Guardians, High Sheriffs, Grand Jurors, and able chairmen? Is not the home-voice of our Julia as the song of a bird, after considerable bow-wowing out of doors?

This, of course, leads straight on to the creation of Mrs Jellyby in *Bleak House* a few months later and the serio-comic description of how she has desolated her home as a result of having, as Conversation Kenge says, 'devoted herself to an extensive variety of public subjects, at various times' (Dickens's depiction of this character enraged that notable early feminist John Stuart Mill: 'that creature Dickens ... has the vulgar impudence ... to ridicule rights of women ... in the very vulgarest way'). Mrs Jellyby's family live in discomfort and disorder while she concentrates on her immense correspondence about Borrioboola-Gha. Dickens, so justly celebrated by Bagehot for his 'endless fecundity in laughter-causing detail', hits upon a marvellous detail to express the invasion and destruction of home by the outside world that results from Mrs Jellyby's 'mission'; presiding at a somewhat chaotic family dinner, she 'received so many letters that Richard, who sat by her, saw four envelopes in the gravy at once' (*BH*, 4).

One of the strongest preservers of Home against the harsh outside world in Dickens's fiction is not female but male, however. This is Wemmick in *Great Expectations*, clerk to that forbidding master of the criminal law, Mr Jaggers. Wemmick determinedly leaves the office behind him when he goes home to his little house in the lowly suburb of Walworth lovingly to tend his 'Aged P.' and to enjoy the society of Miss Skiffins, and he has, as he proudly shows Pip, actually fortified his 'castle' against the outer world by supplying it with a drawbridge to cut off communication (a plank crossing a 'chasm' about four feet wide and two feet deep), and provisioning it to withstand a siege:

> ' — At the back there's a pig, and there are fowls and rabbits; then I knock together my own little frame, you see, and grow cucumbers; and you'll judge at supper what sort of a salad I can raise. So, sir,' said Wemmick, smiling again, but seriously, too, as he shook his head, 'if you can suppose the little place besieged, it would hold out a devil of a time in point of provisions.' (*GE*, 25)

'Provisions.' Again, we notice the emphasis on the provision of food as one of the two essentials of Home in Dickens, the other being, as we have noted, warmth, the fire brightly burning on the hearth. (Both these features, we might note, are prominent in the diabolical counterfeit Home into which Fagin invites *Oliver Twist*, the place where he plans to 'blacken his soul for ever'.)

So far we have been primarily concerned with Dickens's ideal of Home as it affects the individual but there was a strong political aspect to it as well. I quoted in an earlier chapter the farm labourer Will Fern's plea to the gentry in *The Chimes* for the provision of better homes and better food for the poor, who would then be more submissive and governable. Even Dickens's favourite recipe for social progress, public education, depended for its success on the creation, facilitated by government, of true homes among the poor. In his *Household Words* address 'To Working Men' (1854), also cited above, Dickens vigorously re-stated his long-standing conviction, 'founded upon observation', that reform of the poor's housing

> ... must precede all other reforms; and that without it, all other reforms must fail. Neither Religion nor Education

will make any way, in this nineteenth century of Christianity, until a Christian government shall have discharged its first obligation and secured to the people *Homes*, instead of polluted dens. [my italics]

As he says in this piece, Dickens had long urged this point, in both writings and speeches. He made powerful after-dinner speeches at banquets of the Metropolitan Sanitary Association in both 1850 and 1851, asking in the latter,

What avails it to send a Missionary to me, a miserable man or woman living in a foetid Court where every sense bestowed upon me for my delight becomes a torment, and every minute of my life is new mire added to the heap under which I lie degraded? ... I am so surrounded by material filth that my Soul can not rise to the contemplation of an immaterial existence! Or, if I be a miserable child, born and nurtured in the same wretched place, and tempted, in these better times, to the Ragged School, what can the few hours' teaching that I get there do for me against the noxious, constant, ever-renewed lesson of my whole existence.

And one of his most elaborate assertions of the direct link between the homes of the poor and the well-being, and indeed the very security, of the nation occurs in a long authorial intervention in chapter 38 of *The Old Curiosity Shop* (this novel was first published in the format of a cheap weekly miscellany aimed at a mass readership, *Master Humphrey's Clock*, 1840-41). After stressing that Kit Nubbles's strong love for his humble home has not been at all altered by his comfortable situation as the Garlands' live-in servant, Dickens has the following excursus:

The ties that bind the wealthy and the proud to home may be forged on earth, but those which link the poor man to his humble hearth are of the truer metal and bear the stamp of Heaven .... . His household gods are of flesh and blood, with no alloy of silver, gold, or precious stone; he has no property but in the affections of his own heart; and when they endear bare floors and walls, despite of rags and toil and scanty fare, that man has his love of home from God, and his rude hut becomes a solemn place.

Oh! if only those who rule the destinies of nations would but remember this – if they would but think how hard it is for the very poor to have engendered in their hearts, that love of home from which all domestic virtues spring, when they live in dense and squalid masses where social decency is lost, or rather never found, ... if they would ... strive to improve the wretched dwellings in bye-ways where only Poverty may walk, – many low roofs would point more truly to the sky, than the loftiest steeple that now rears proudly up from the midst of guilt, and crime, and horrible disease, to mock them by its contrast. It is no light matter .... In love of home, the love of country has its rise; and who are the truer patriots or the better in time of need – those who venerate the land, owning its wood, and stream, and earth, and all that they produce? or those who love their country, boasting not a foot of ground in all its wide domain!

The homes of the poor are here presented not only as the best and truest altars in the country but also as bulwarks of the nation; Dickens makes them, in fact, the equivalent of that other grand traditional symbol of national security, the British tar, guardian of England's 'wooden walls' (earlier, Douglas Jerrold had skilfully combined the two things, humble home and heroic tar, in his *Black Eyed Susan* [1829] which goes a long way towards explaining the enormous and enduring popularity of this particular play throughout the period).

Dickens was not, of course, only responding to the spirit of

the age, domestic and progressive, in his idealisation of Home.
With him it was an intensely personal sentiment too. In *My
Father As I Recall Him* (1896) his elder daughter Mamie (who
helped her aunt, Georgina Hogarth, to run his home after the
break-up of the marriage) elaborated on his 'home-loving'
nature calling him 'a "home man" in every respect'; and repeated (without acknowledgment) Forster's judgment that 'no
man was so inclined naturally to derive his happiness from
home affairs'. Mamie does not, however, quote Forster's explanation for this passion for home. Referring to Dickens's
'childish sufferings', Forster writes (XI. 3) of 'the sense they
burnt into him of the misery of loneliness and a craving for the
joys of home'. There can be little doubt of the truth of this and
Dickens's finest and most insightful modern biographer, Peter
Ackroyd, is absolutely right when he comments: 'Dickens's
acute sense of, and need for "Home" … sprang from his own
experience of being banished from that blessed place' (an
experience most poignantly dramatised in the early chapters of
David Copperfield).

What also seems quite personal to him, and no doubt has its
roots in his interpretation of his childhood experiences, is the
frequency with which wives and mothers appear in his novels
as home-wreckers rather than as home-makers. We meet in his
books, from Mrs Nickleby and Mrs Vardon (*BR*) onwards
through to Mrs Joe (*GE*), Mrs Wilfer (*OMF*), and the mother of
George Silverman, a whole succession of incompetent or weak
or foolish or ill-tempered women who make home anything but
a place of peace and spiritual refreshment for their families.
With Dickens home-makers are more likely to be sisters and
daughters, like Ruth Pinch (*MC*) and Little Dorrit. Even that
paragon wife Dot Peerybingle seems much more daughterly
than wifely in her relationship to Old John, the 'very doll of a
baby' notwithstanding, and Dickens's supreme embodiment of
the Angel in the House, Agnes Wickfield in *Copperfield*,
spends nearly all the novel being daughterly to her father (he

calls her his 'little housekeeper') and sisterly to David, figuring as a wife only in the novel's last two chapters.

Given Dickens's intense *personal* investment in the concept of Home, the other side of the coin, Homelessness, was, naturally enough, an equally intense preoccupation of his, both in his personal and in his public life, and it features prominently in his writings. The securely-based, home-loving, intensely familial Dickens had as his alter ego the Dickens that needed to roam and wander — always conscious, however, that such 'vagabondage', however compulsive, was 'amateur', that is, undertaken as a matter of choice not of bleak necessity and actual homelessness. He was haunted by what might have happened to him as a result of the spectacular failure of Home in his childhood, after his father had been taken to prison, leaving his wife and children briefly 'encamped' in an 'emptied house' before they joined him in the prison ('I really believed that they had broken my heart', Dickens wrote in his abortive autobiography):

> I know that I have lounged about the streets, insuffi-
> ciently and unsatisfactorily fed. I know that, but for the
> mercy of God, I might easily have been, for any care that
> was taken of me, a little robber or a little vagabond.
> (Forster, I. 2)

Forster appends a footnote to his discussion (VIII. 2) of Dickens's state of extreme restlessness during 1857-58 which also touches on Dickens's sense of the very different life that he might have led:

> Anything more completely opposed to the Micawber
> type could hardly be conceived, yet there were moments
> (really and truly only moments) when the fancy would
> arise that if the conditions of his life had been reversed,
> something of a vagabond existence (using the word in

Goldsmith's meaning [see ch. 20 of *The Vicar of Wakefield*, 'The History of a Philosophic Vagabond']) might have supervened. It would have been an unspeakable misery to him, but it might have come nevertheless.

But Dickens also knew, and said in his account of his 'hard experiences in boyhood' that he knew, 'how all these things have worked together to make me what I am'; he was well aware of how much his childhood wanderings in the streets of London had sharpened his extraordinary powers of minute observation, as well as stimulating and enriching the life of his 'fancy'. And the possibility to indulge in 'vagabondage' remained essential to him as an artist throughout his life. It lies at the heart of his greatest essay-writing in *The Uncommercial Traveller*, where he adopts the persona of 'Mr Traveller' who is 'always on the road', and in one of the *Uncommercial* pieces, 'Shy Neighbourhoods' (*ATYR*, 26 May 1860) he distinguishes between the two kinds of walking he practises:

> ... one, straight on end to a definite goal at round pace [this is the one used when 'Mr Traveller' is in his investigative-journalist mode]; one, objectless, loitering, and purely vagabond. In the latter state, no gipsy on earth is a greater vagabond than myself; it is so natural to me, and strong with me, that I think I must be the descendant, at no great distance, of some irreclaimable tramp.

It is, he continues, 'in a vagabond course of shy [i. e., dubious, disreputable] metropolitan neighbourhoods and shops' that he made the observations of animal behaviour that are described with such a rich abundance of fancy and imagination in the essay that follows.

The first fruits of Dickens's talent for 'vagabondage' had appeared nearly thirty years earlier, in *Sketches by Boz* and we find in the first published version of one of the sketches, 'The

Prisoner's Van' (*Bell's Life in London*, 29 Nov. 1835), that 'Boz' comments directly on this behaviour-pattern – using, we notice, one of the very phrases that later appeared, to such very different effect, in the autobiographical fragment in Forster:

> We have a most extraordinary partiality for lounging about the streets. Whenever we have an hour or two to spare, there is nothing we enjoy more than a little amateur vagrancy – walking up one street and down another, and staring into shop windows, and gazing about as if, instead of being on intimate terms with every shop and house in Holborn, the Strand, Fleet-street and Cheapside, the whole were an unknown region to our wandering mind.

His first sustained narrative, *The Pickwick Papers*, is a novel all about wandering, with a hero determined not 'to gaze on Goswell Street for ever' but to roam about England with a small band of friends in search of new knowledge and experiences. His faithful servant, and to a large extent mentor, is that veteran of 'vagabond' street life, Sam Weller whose father proudly tells Mr Pickwick (in a fascinating echo of Dickens's own father's response, as reported by Dickens himself, to a question asking him where his son had been educated: 'Why, indeed, Sir – ha! ha! – he may be said to have educated himself!')

> 'I took a good deal o' pains with his eddication, sir: let him run in the streets when he was wery young, and shift for his-self. It's the only way to make a boy sharp, sir.' (*PP*, 20)

In *Nicholas Nickleby* comes some enforced vagabondage when the young-gentleman hero experiences a reversal of fortune quite as dramatic as the child Dickens's had been. Like Goldsmith's 'philosophic vagabond', he becomes a temporary member of a troupe of strolling players (later, Dickens himself took great delight in seeing himself and his Amateur Players, travelling to perform in different cities, as 'strollers'). Then Master Humphrey, whose custom it is to wander 'by night and day, at all hours and seasons, in city streets and quiet country parts', introduces Dickens's second great novel of wandering, *The Old Curiosity Shop* in which Nell and her half-crazed grandfather are forced into a very strange kind of 'vagabond-age', as also are Barnaby Rudge and his mother and his pet raven in the novel following that. But all this picaresque-type of 'open road' wandering, whether forced or unforced and motivated by benevolent interest in the world like Pickwick's or Humphrey's, disappears from the novels after 1842 and Dickens's own devastating experience of a six-month period of a rather different kind of itinerant 'homelessness', the sort involved in a six-month celebrity tour in the United States, a country that proved to be a good deal more alien than he had anticipated. (One must add here, though, to keep things in proportion, that his whole approach to his art was also changing and developing at this time as he consciously sought, from *Martin Chuzzlewit* onwards, to structure his novels more care-fully and to give them a unity greater than that of characters travelling the open road.)

From *Chuzzlewit* onwards journeys have definite goals. Martin and Mark travel to America for a purpose, young David Copperfield runs away to Dover for a purpose, Mr Peggotty sets out to wander across Europe for a purpose, and it is not until we come to old Betty Higden in *Our Mutual Friend*, desperately taking to a life of wandering to escape the dreaded workhouse, that we have again a Nell-type situation of enforced and aimless wandering. The only truly 'vagabond' traveller would seem to be the predatory villain Rigaud, alias Blandois, in *Little Dorrit*, and Dickens seems to conceive him more as some kind of Mephistophelean devil-figure (going about seeking whom he may devour) than as a normal human character. But we should note the special, and glorious, case of the Micawbers in *David*

Copperfield who combine something very close to vagabond-age with what is elsewhere in Dickens its complete opposite, intense domesticity. As their encampment in Windsor Terrace is being broken up and David, who has become very much one of the family, acts as the Micawbers' emissary to the pawn-broker's, Mrs Micawber continues to arrange little domestic 'treats', generally in the form of a cosy family supper, and David finds 'something gipsy-like and agreeable' in the dinner he later shares with Mr Micawber in the debtor's prison. Wher-ever Mr Micawber goes, whether into the King's Bench, or on quasi-buccaneering forays into the provinces, he goes very much *en famille*; and even if the children have sometimes to be left behind in lodgings, Mrs Micawber is always by his side:

> 'He is the parent of my children! He is the father of my twins! He is the husband of my affections,' cried Mrs Micawber, struggling; 'and I ne – ver – will – desert Mr Micawber!' (*DC*, 12)

Eventually the Micawbers, too, become purposeful travel-lers, emigrating to Australia along with the Peggotty menage, but during the early part of *Copperfield* at least they are both peripatetic *and* domestic.

'Vagabond' travelling may no longer feature in Dickens's novels and stories after 1842 but the homeless certainly do, especially women and children. One thinks of, among others, the 'savage' child in *The Haunted Man*, also the unnamed prostitute Redlaw encounters in that book; of Martha in *David Copperfield* and Jo in *Bleak House* who lives ('that is to say, Jo has not yet died') in one of the 'ruined shelters' in the 'black, dilapidated street' of Tom-all-Alone's; the prostitute who speaks to Little Dorrit and Maggy when they have to spend the night on the streets, shrinking past 'homeless people coiled up in nooks' and participating in 'the shame, desertion, wretched-ness, and exposure, of the great capital' (*LD*, I. 14); and the 'some half-dozen people [who] had lately died in the street of starvation', mention of whom in polite society makes Mr Podsnap so angry in *Our Mutual Friend* (I. 11). Prostitutes feature largely in this list – appropriately enough because they did in real life form a substantial section of London's street-wanderers – and the most prolonged and intensive charitable effort of Dickens's life was that concerned with trying to 'reclaim' some of these women and turn them to domesticity. For several years he was the active supervisor of the significantly-named 'Home for Homeless Women' established by Miss Coutts at Shepherd's Bush. He wrote a pamphlet headed an 'Appeal' to be given to female prisoners in which he speaks of the decision to set up 'a HOME' for those who wished to change their lives and how they would in this Home 'be taught all household work that would be useful to them in a home of their own and enable them to make it comfortable and happy' (such women as they hoped to reclaim, he told Miss Coutts, had to be '*tempted* into virtue').

Dickens also wrote a long article on Miss Coutts's Home for *Household Words* in 1853 and three years later again featured homeless women in the journal with a powerful piece entitled 'A Nightly Scene in London' (26 Jan. 1856). This describes five women, first perceived as 'five bundles of rags', that he had stumbled across one wretched November night outside the workhouse in Whitechapel after he and a companion had 'strayed' into that deprived district. The women were squatting there in the soaking rain, 'five great beehives covered with rags', because there was no room for them in the casual ward. Having ascertained this to be true, Dickens gives each of the women money to find a night's lodging. (His account of the event savagely attacks the Utilitarian political economists, 'unreasonable disciples of a reasonable school', who would 'easily prove that such things ought to be, and that no man has any business to mind them'.)

But Dickens's most powerful evocation of ultimate home-

lessness appears in an Uncommercial Traveller essay, already
cited above. In 'Night Walks' (*ATYR*, 21 July 1860) he recalls
a period when he suffered from insomnia and would get up and
roam all night about the city acquiring thereby 'a fair amateur
experience of houselessness'. He, in fact, becomes the very
embodiment of this quality, referring to himself as 'Houselessness' throughout the essay as he describes his solitary
wanderings in the dark city and 'the yearning of the houseless
mind ... for any sign of company, any lighted place, any
movement, anything suggestive of anyone being up ... '. One
night Amateur Houselessness has a startlingly close encounter
with the real thing:

> I came to the great steps of St Martin's church as the
> clock was striking Three. Suddenly, a thing that in a
> moment more I should have trodden upon without see-
> ing, rose up at my feet with a cry of loneliness and
> houselessness, struck out of it by the bell, the like of
> which I never heard. We then stood face to face looking
> at one another, frightened by one another. The creature
> was like a beetle-browed hair-lipped youth of twenty,
> and it had a loose bundle of rags on, which it held
> together with one of its hands. It shivered from head to
> foot, and its teeth chattered, and as it stared at me –
> persecutor, devil, ghost, whatever it thought me – it made
> with its whining mouth as if it were snapping at me like
> a worried dog. Intending to give this ugly object money,
> I put out my hand to stay it – for it recoiled as it whined
> and snapped – and laid my hand upon its shoulder.
> Instantly, it twisted out of its garment, like the young man
> in the New Testament, and left me standing alone with its
> rags in my hand.

As in the case of the street child in *The Haunted Man*, used
to being 'worried and hunted like a beast', or the Irish 'men,

women, children' shown to Dickens by Inspector Field in a cheap lodging-house, 'for the most part naked, heaped upon the floor like maggots in a cheese' (*RP*), or the fighting beggar-brats in 'On An Amateur Beat' (*UT*), or the vermin-like creatures that swarm 'in maggot numbers' in the 'ruined shelters' of Tom-all-Alone's, Dickens describes the homeless youth he stumbles across as repulsively sub-human (the allusion to the New Testament perhaps hints at the quasi-blasphemous horror of finding such a figure in the streets of a great and supposedly Christian city). The animal imagery helps convey to readers the strength of Dickens's good-citizenly (and Christian) horror and indignation at society's toleration of such sights in the streets of the nation's capital. But there is, I think, also an element of *personal* horror involved for Dickens, haunted as we know he was by the idea of that 'little vagabond' that he believed he might so easily have become.

*

Addressing the anniversary dinner of the Commercial Travellers' Schools in December 1854, Dickens observed

> Every traveller has a home of his own, and he learns to appreciate it the more from his wandering. [*Cheers.*] If he has no home, he learns the same lesson unselfishly by turning to the homes of other men. He may have his experiences of cheerful and exciting pleasures abroad; but home is best, after all, and its pleasures are the most heartily and enduringly prized. [*Loud cheers.*]

He had certainly proved the truth of this upon his pulses during his tour of America in 1842. For six months this intensely home-loving man had been, together with his wife, far away from his children and his 'household gods', staying in hotel after hotel, meeting endless strangers ('I suppose we shook hands, before going to bed, with considerably more than five hundred people') including many intrusively curious ones ('I get out at a station, and can't drink a glass of water, without having a hundred people looking down my throat when I open my mouth to swallow'), and constantly on the move, by train or canal-boat or steamboat. Towards the end of the tour Catherine and he were suffering agonies of homesickness (for the rest of his life Dickens would sometimes be troubled by a dream in which he was wandering in America and unable to find his way home) and he was no doubt remembering their feelings on finally getting back to England when he came to describe the exultation of Martin Chuzzlewit and Mark Tapley returning to England after their disastrous American expedition, and rejoicing in their first sight of 'the old churches, roofs and darkened chimney-stacks of Home'. This chapter may fittingly end with a quotation from Dickens's last letter to Forster from America (Forster, III. 7):

> As the time draws nearer we get FEVERED with anxiety for home ... Kiss our darlings for us. We shall soon meet, please God, and be happier and merrier than ever we were in all our lives ... Oh home – home – home – home – home – home – HOME !!!!!!!!!!!

Faith

> I commit my soul to the mercy of God through our Lord
> and Saviour Jesus Christ, and I exhort my dear children
> humbly to try to guide themselves by the teaching of the
> New Testament in its broad spirit, and to put no faith in
> any man's narrow construction of its letter here or there.
>
> From Dickens's Will

In his *Diary of A Writer* (1876) Dostoevsky refers to Dickens
as 'the great Christian', and most of his British readers (not
including John Ruskin, however) would certainly also have
seen him in such terms. But it is, as has been often pointed out,
by no means easy to define Dickens's particular brand of
Christianity, at any point in his career. Forster, when recording
Dickens's temporary adherence to Unitarianism (of which
more below), hastened to add:

> But upon essential points he had never any sympathy so
> strong as with the leading doctrines of the Church of
> England; to these, as time went on, he found himself able
> to accommodate all minor differences; and the unswerv-
> ing faith in Christianity itself, apart from sects and
> schisms, which had never failed him at any period of his
> life, found expression at its close in the language of his
> will. (Forster, IV. 1)

He then quotes the passage reproduced as an epigraph to this
chapter. But, of course, such generalised phrases as 'essential

points', 'leading doctrines' and 'minor differences', as well as what might be meant by 'Christianity itself ', left people very little wiser about just what it was that Dostoevsky's 'great Christian' did believe. Unsurprisingly, it led to 'much questioning', as Forster put it, and he felt obliged to return to the subject in the last chapter (entitled 'Personal Characteristics') of the penultimate Book of his biography, and, as we shall see below, once more to bring in Dickens's own voice in an attempt to clarify the situation.

However hard it may be to define the precise nature of Dickens's religious faith, no reader can fail to be very much aware of the recurrent *flavour* of religion that is found throughout all his writings. This is partly, but only partly, the result of his many Biblical allusions, or use of Biblical language (often, it should be noted, for comic effect as in the case of Mrs Gamp's splendidly gnomic Scriptural utterances, e. g., 'Rich folk may ride on camels but it ain't so easy for 'em to see out of a needle's eye'). A good example of Dickens's serious use of Scriptural allusion occurs in chapter 18 of *Dombey and Son* after Florence Dombey has been described as being agonised with grief over the death of her little brother:

> But it is not in the nature of pure love to burn so fiercely and unkindly long. The flame that in its grosser composition has the taint of earth, may prey upon the breast that gives it shelter; but the sacred fire from heaven is as gentle in the heart, as when it rested on the heads of the assembled twelve, and showed each man his brother, brightened and unhurt. The image conjured up, there soon returned the placid face, the softened voice, the loving looks, the quiet trustfulness and peace; and Florence, though she wept still, wept more tranquilly, and courted the remembrance.

Dickens here takes a detail from the New Testament account of the miracle of the first Whitsun or the Speaking in Tongues (the gift of the Holy Ghost to the apostles) and uses it for his novelistic purpose, namely to express the part that her 'quiet trustfulness' in God played in comforting the bereaved girl. The reader is not encouraged to dwell on how appropriate in detail this Biblical allusion may be but receives a strong impression of a generalised Christian message (compare also the passage about the young man in the New Testament who fled without his garment quoted above, pp. 150, from 'Night Walks').

Three of Dickens's novels seem particularly suffused with this kind of message. In *Oliver Twist* (1837-38), *The Old Curiosity Shop* (1840-41) and *Little Dorrit* (1855-57), both the main plot or story-line and the major characters seem to be charged with definite religious significance. It is hinted at in the Bunyanesque sub-title of Oliver, 'the parish boy's progress', and spelled out in the 1846 preface to the 'Third edition' of the novel: 'I wished to show, in little Oliver, the principle of Good surviving through every adverse circumstance, and triumphing at last'. Echoes of *The Pilgrim's Progress* are heard again in *The Old Curiosity Shop* when Nell and her grandfather flee the city where the evil Quilp seems all-powerful to 'travel afoot through the fields and woods ... and trust [themselves] to God in the places where He dwells', finding at last a haven of sanctuary attached to an old church where Nell, who has all along been so much possessed by death, finally dies a sanctified death (George Cattermole's tailpiece illustration to the novel shows her being wafted heavenwards by angels bearing harps and lilies):

'It is not,' said the schoolmaster, as he bent down to kiss her on the cheek and give his tears free vent, 'it is not on earth that Heaven's justice ends. Think what earth is, compared with that World to which her young spirit has winged its early flight; and say if one deliberate wish expressed in solemn terms above this bed could call her back to life, which one of us would utter it!' (*OCS*, 71)

Little Dorrit (once famously interpreted by Lionel Trilling as Dickens's version of 'the Beatrice of the [*Divine*] *Comedy*, the Paraclete in female form') does not die at the end of the book but marries Clennam, the man she has loved so long and whom she has redeemed from despair. They marry in the church in which she was christened 'with the sun shining on them through the painted figure of Our Saviour on the window', and go down, 'inseparable and blessed', into 'the roaring streets'. The novel ends with one of Dickens's most impressive uses of Biblical cadence as he describes the crowded streets where 'the noisy and the eager, and the arrogant and the froward and the vain, fretted and chafed, and made their usual uproar'.

I have highlighted *Oliver Twist*, *The Old Curiosity Shop* and *Little Dorrit* as the three novels that seem to be the ones most thoroughly suffused with religious meaning but, as I have said, Biblical allusions and the use of Biblical language occur throughout Dickens's writings, and it is a rare commentator on his death who fails to point out, following Forster, that almost the last words he penned in the chapter of *Edwin Drood* he was writing on the day he was taken fatally ill describe a 'brilliant morning' shining on the ancient city of Cloisterham, and the 'changes of glorious light' (the same light that he had long before called 'creation's mind' in *The Old Curiosity Shop*) that 'penetrate into the Cathedral, subdue its earthy odour, and preach the Resurrection and the Life'. Earlier in the same novel, however, came a nice example of Dickens using Scriptural imagery for comic effect (admittedly, an image that had passed into the language and become very hackneyed, which is the point of the joke) and this had given offence to a certain Mr J. M. Makeham who wrote to remonstrate. The offending passage runs as follows:

Into this herbaceous penitentiary [his mother's medicine-
room] ... would the Reverend Septimus submissively be
led, like the highly-popular lamb who has so long and
unresistingly been led to the slaughter, and there would
he, unlike that lamb, bore nobody but himself. (*MED*, 10)

Mr Makeham must have reminded Dickens that the 'highly-
popular lamb' had first made his appearance in the Book of
Isaiah (53. 5) and was generally held to be prophetic of Christ
being taken to be crucified. It was Dickens's reply, written the
day before he died, that Forster calls in evidence (XI. 3) when
he feels he has to return to the question of Dickens's Christian
faith. Dickens told Makeham that he was 'truly shocked' that
any reader 'could possibly attach such a scriptural reference' to
his use of 'a much abused social figure of speech', and went on
to say:

I have always striven in my writings to express venera-
tion for the life and lessons of Our Saviour; because I feel
it; and because I re-wrote that history for my children —
every one of whom knew it, from having it repeated to
them — long before they could read, and almost as soon
as they could speak.

But I have never made proclamation of this from the
house-tops.

Forster also refers the reader to Dickens's earlier correspondence (1861) with the Rev. David Macrae, published by
Macrae in a book called *Home and Abroad* (1871). Here we
find a fuller, but still quite generalised, statement by Dickens
concerning the religious element in his work:

With a deep sense of my great responsibility always upon
me when I exercise my art, one of my most constant and

most earnest endeavours has been to exhibit in all my good people some faint reflections of the teachings of our great Master, and unostentatiously to lead the reader up to those teachings as the great source of all moral goodness. All my strongest illustrations are derived from the New Testament; all my social abuses are shown as departures from its spirit; all my good people are humble, charitable, faithful and forgiving. Over and over again, I claim them in express words as disciples of the Founder of our religion; but I must admit that to a man (or woman) they all arise and wash their faces, and do not appear unto men to fast. [Dickens is here referring to Matthew 6, 16-18 where Christ warns his followers against hypocritical outward shows of piety]

Dennis Walder, reprinting this correspondence in *The Dickensian* (Spring 1985), notes that it seems to contain some over-statement. It is not easy to find examples of Dickens's heroes or heroines being described 'in express words' as followers of Christ, though it is certainly the case with Little Dorrit when she appeals to Mrs Clennam to put aside her Old Testament beliefs about vengeance and punishment (*LD*, II. 31). But what Dickens writes in this letter does nevertheless carry entire conviction as a statement of how he saw himself and his work, from the standpoint of religion.

The apparently very generalised nature of Dickens's Christianity (how he actually understood or interpreted the doctrine of the Resurrection, for example) was a decided advantage to him as a hugely popular artist, living as he did during a period of intense and often embittered religious controversy (Low Church versus High Church, Evangelicals versus Ritualists or Tractarians, church versus chapel, and so on). It promoted what one reviewer of *Little Dorrit* quoted by Philip Collins in his *Dickens: the Critical Heritage* saw as a Shakespeare-like 'feeling of universal sympathy with human nature which breathes through all his pages like the "broad and general" atmosphere':

> He soars above all considerations of sect, above all nar-
> row isolations of creed; and, though a more deeply
> religious writer is not to be found, in all those elements
> of religion which rise eternally from the natural emotions
> of love and reverence, he is never disputatiously theo-
> logical or academically dogmatic.

Dickens deplored any religious movement that seemed to be more concerned with forms of worship and controversy about that than with helping what George Eliot once called 'poor stricken humanity'. 'I find I am getting horribly bitter about Puseyism', he wrote to Albany Fonblanque on 13 March 1843: 'Good God to talk in these times of most untimely ignorance among the people, about what Priests shall wear, and whither they shall turn when they say their prayers … '. As we have noted above (p. 114) he satirised 'Puseyism', a contemptuous term for the Oxford Movement derived from the name of one of its leading figures, in his 'Report of the Commissioners Appointed to Inquire into the Condition of the Persons Vari-ously Engaged in the University of Oxford', published anonymously in Fonblanque's weekly *The Examiner* (3 June 1843):

> A vast number of witnesses being interrogated as to what
> they understood by the words Religion and Salvation,
> answered Lighted Candles. Some said water; some
> bread; others, little boys; others mixed the water, lighted
> candles, bread and little boys all up together, and called
> the compound Faith.

Shortly afterwards, Dickens wrote a poem with the title 'A

Word in Season' for his friend Lady Blessington's annual, *The Keepsake*. In it he describes England as a country where

> ... brutal ignorance, and toil, and dearth
> Were the hard portion of its sons and daughters:
> And yet, where they who should have oped the door
> Of charity and light for all men's finding
> Squabbled for words upon the altar-floor,
> And rent The Book, in struggles for the binding.

And at the end of 'A Sleep to Startle Us' (*HW*, 13 March 1852) he turns on the Church of England, still much exercised both about Puseyism and the Gorham controversy (Gorham was an Anglican clergyman whom the High Church Bishop of Exeter had refused to induct into his parish because of his Calvinist views):

> Dearly beloved brethren ..., do you know that between Gorham controversies, and Pusey controversies and Newman controversies, and twenty other edifying controversies, a certain large class of minds in the community is gradually being driven out of all religion! Would it be well, do you think, to come down out of the controversies for a little while, and be simply Apostolic thus low down [i. e., in the Ragged School night-refuge for homeless men and boys]!

Shortly afterwards, he began work on *Bleak House* in which novel he introduces a scathing denunciation, through the dying words of the hapless Jo, of sectarian squabbling taking precedence over true Christian concern for the poor and ignorant. Asked if he knows any prayers, Jo replies that he does not, even though he and his fellow slum-dwellers had been visited by clergymen and preachers:

Different times, there wos other genlmen come down
Tom-all-Alone's a-prayin,' but they all mostly sed as the
t'other wuns prayed wrong, and all mostly sounded to be
a-talkin to theirselves, or a-passin blame on the t'others,
and not a-talkin to us. We never knowd nothink. I never
knowd what it wos all about. (*BH*, 47)

Dickens himself, however, as we have seen with regard to
his satire on the Oxford Movement, was not behind-hand in
attacking certain fellow-Christians who 'prayed wrong', most
notably those two polar opposites among contemporary sects or
denominations, the Evangelicals (whether within or without the
Church of England) and the Roman Catholics (together with
the Puseyites, whom he and many others regarded as merely
fellow-travellers of the Catholics). The Evangelicals offended
him on theological as well as on social, moral and aesthetic
grounds; his objections to Catholicism had more to do with
hatred of 'priestcraft', and what he saw as the Church's consis-
tent, and often brutal, suppression of individual freedoms and
its opposition to the progressive spirit of the age, and its attempts to keep its followers in a state of degraded and
dependent ignorance. There was also a strong John Bull-ish
streak in Dickens which would have predisposed him against
any church in England owing allegiance to a foreign potentate.
His description of the faces of the priests and monks in the
streets of Genoa ('If Nature's handwriting be at all legible,
greater varieties of sloth, deceit, and intellectual torpor, could
hardly be observed among any class of men in the world' while
Jesuits 'slink noiselessly about, in pairs, like black cats') is
characteristic of that strong vein of anti-Catholicism that runs
through *Pictures from Italy* and probably caused Dickens's
much-loved friend, the painter Clarkson Stanfield, who was a
Catholic, to give up the commission he had accepted to illus-
trate the work.

It was in Genoa that Dickens had an extraordinary, and

extraordinarily vivid, dream of being visited by a Madonna-like figure, swathed in blue drapery, that, he told Forster, he recognised as the spirit of his dead sister-in-law Mary Hogarth, 'so full of compassion and sorrow for me ... that it cut me to the heart'. After beseeching this figure for some token that it had really visited him and being promised a sign, Dickens asked 'in an agony of entreaty' lest the Spirit should vanish

> 'What is the True religion?' As it paused a moment without replying, I said — Good God in such an agony of haste, lest it should go away! — 'You think, as I do, that the Form of religion does not so greatly matter, if we try to do good? — or,' I said, observing that it still hesitated, and was moved with the greatest compassion for me, 'perhaps the Roman Catholic is the best? Perhaps it makes one think of God oftener, and believe in him more steadily?' 'For you,' said the Spirit, full of such heavenly tenderness for me, that I felt as if my heart would break; 'for you, it is the best!' Then I awoke, with the tears running down my face, and myself in exactly the condition of the dream. (Forster, IV. 5)

Biographical commentators have naturally had a field day with this, linking Dickens's own personal 'Mariolatry' with the Mariolatry by which he found himself surrounded in Genoa. The really strange thing about it all, as Forster's account certainly implies, is that it seems to have had no effect whatever on the nature of Dickens's religious faith, and certainly did not at all abate his hostility to Roman Catholicism which, as just mentioned, comes out particularly strongly in the next book he wrote, *Pictures From Italy*. Despite the intensity with which he describes this dream, and its all-important subject-matter, Dickens seems more interested, at least in the portion of the letter quoted by Forster, in arriving at a psychological rather than a spiritual interpretation of the experience. 'I wonder whether I should regard it as a dream or an actual Vision!' he writes. Presumably, he decided it was only a dream and not a spiritual message directing a particular course of action. Forster calls it a 'disturbing fancy', and comments that it forms part of much evidence to be found in Dickens's life of his 'not having escaped those trying regions of reflection which most men of thought and all men of genius have at some time to pass through'. Forster is referring, presumably, to that dread intellectual phenomenon known to Victorian Christians as 'Doubt'. He goes on to say that the book which helped Dickens most to come through this period was A. P. Stanley's life of Dr. Arnold, the great Headmaster of Rugby School and champion of 'Broad Church' Anglicanism. Forster's review of this work moved Dickens to write, 'I must have that book. Every sentence that you quote from it is the text-book of my faith'. It was most likely that the Broad Church movement with its broad and liberal interpretation of formularies and rubrics, and its openness towards scientific discoveries kept Dickens in the Church of England; and it was appropriate that it was Stanley who should have preached a sermon in Westminster Abbey celebrating Dickens's life and work shortly after his death.

Returning to Dickens's hostility towards Evangelical Christians, biographers have sometimes sought to account for this on personal grounds, largely on the basis of a passage in 'City of London Churches' (*UT*), assumed (on no evidence whatever) to be literally autobiographical (in the passage the Traveller recalls how often in his early childhood he was dragged to a chapel and for two hours 'steamed like a potato in the unventilated breath of the powerful [preacher] Boanerges Boiler and his congregation'). But there really is no need to look for a biographical explanation. Many things about the Evangelical brand of Christianity would have been anathema to Dickens with his fundamental beliefs in a beneficent and infinitely loving Deity, in Nature as expressive of such a God, and in the innocence of childhood (it is, I think, more profitable to speculate on how much this latter belief may owe to a reading of Wordsworth than to search for an original for Boanerges Boiler). Evangelicals tended to lay emphasis on the, to Dickens, utterly repellent doctrine of Original Sin and innate human depravity. 'The gloomy theology of the Murdstones', David Copperfield tells us, 'made all children out to be a swarm of little vipers (though there was a child once set in the midst of the Disciples)'. In *Oliver Twist* Dickens not only embodies 'the principle of Good' in the figure of a child but he also challengingly makes little Oliver doubly 'a child of sin' in the eyes of Murdstonian Christians by making him illegitimate. Also illegitimate is Esther Summerson in *Bleak House*, horrified to be told by her Calvinist 'godmother' (actually her aunt) that she was not born, like other children, 'in common sin and wrathfulness' but is 'set apart' and must 'pray daily that the sins of others be not visited upon [her] head, according to what is written' (referring to Exodus 20. 5: 'for I thy God am a jealous God, visiting the iniquity of the fathers upon the children unto the third and fourth generation of them that hate me'). Arthur Clennam in *Little Dorrit*, another love-child, has been 'brought up in fear and trembling' by his stern putative mother, in, as she puts it, 'a life of practical contrition for the sins that were heavy on his head before his entrance into this condemned world'. As a child he was compelled to pass 'dreary Sundays' sitting 'scared out of his senses by a horrible tract which commenced business with the poor child by asking him in its title, why he was going to Perdition?'

Christians of the Murdstone/Mrs Clennam stamp with their grim reliance on the teachings of the Old Testament rather than the New, and their insistence on the sinfulness of human nature and the certainty of Divine retribution, represent Dickens's serious critique of Evangelicalism which for its practicioners is, according to Dr Chillip in *Copperfield* (here very much functioning as a mouthpiece for Dickens), too often merely 'a vent for their bad humours and arrogance'. There is, the mild little doctor observes and David agrees, 'no authority for Mr and Miss Murdstone in the New Testament'. And it is the New Testament, especially the 'beneficent history' of Christ's life and ministry as recorded in the Gospels, that Dickens's religious faith is based upon. In his notes for writing the chapter (*LD*, II. 31) in which *Little Dorrit* appeals to Mrs Clennam to abandon her clinging to the Old Testament as her spiritual guide appear the words: 'Set the darkness and vengeance against the New Testament'. 'Half the misery and hypocrisy of the Christian world arises (as I take it)', Dickens wrote to Frank Stone on 13 December 1858, 'from a stubborn determination to refuse the New Testament as a sufficient guide in itself, and to force the Old Testament into alliance with it – whereof comes all manner of camel-swallowing and gnat-straining'

Dickens was also very much alive to the class aspect of many of the favourite social causes vehemently espoused by Evangelical Christianity as a result of its condemnation of all worldly pleasures as essentially sinful – Sabbatarianism, for example. Dickens was an ardent and lifelong campaigner against politicians like Sir Andrew Agnew or Lord Robert Grosvenor who repeatedly sought to bring in Sunday Observance legislation that would restrict or abolish the 'innocent' pleasures, relaxations and conveniences available to the working classes on a Sunday while leaving the rich unaffected. His pamphlet *Sunday Under Three Heads. As It Is. As Sabbath Bills Would Make It. As It Might Be Made* (1836) details the ways in which the class bias would work and scorns the idea that 'the wise and benificent Creator' could ever have intended that those who work the hardest should be 'debarred from happiness and enjoyment'. In *Nicholas Nickleby* we get a thumbnail sketch of an M.P. Mr Gallanbile who is 'devoted to the Observance question' through the wording of his advertisement for a cook:

No victuals whatever cooked on the Lord's Day with the exception of dinner for Mr and Mrs Gallanbile, which,

being a work of piety and necessity, is exempted. Mr
Gallanbile dines late on the day of rest to prevent the
sinfulness of the cook's dressing herself. (*NN*, 16)

When Arthur Clennam returns to London on a gloomy
Sunday after many years abroad he sees everything

> ... bolted and barred that could by possibility furnish
> relief to an overworked people. No pictures, no unfamil-
> iar animals, no rare plants or flowers, no natural or
> artificial wonders of the ancient world – all *taboo* with
> that enlightened strictness that the ugly South Sea gods
> in the British Museum might have supposed themselves
> at home again... . Nothing for the spent toiler to do but
> to compare the monotony of his seventh day with the
> monotony of his six days ... . (*LD*, I. 3)

Dickens's third great objection to the Evangelical brand of
Christianity, apart from theological and social considerations,
seems to have related to the kind of rhetoric favoured by the
Rev. Boanerges Boiler and his ilk (we are not actually treated
to a specimen of the Rev. Melchisedech Howler's oratory in
Dombey but Dickens more than makes up for it with Chad-
band's flights of dazzling verbosity in *Bleak House*). In *Sunday
Under Three Heads* Dickens depicts a Bible-thumping (literally) preacher spouting 'an extempore prayer, in which he calls
upon the Sacred Founder of the Christian Faith to bless his
ministry in terms of disgusting and impious familiarity not to
be described'. He makes a similar point when defending his
portrayal of Stiggins in his 1847 Preface to *Pickwick*, when he
deplores 'that coarse familiarity with sacred things which is
busy on the lip, and idle in the heart' (no wonder Dickens was
so shocked by Mr Makeham's letter). For him the truths of the
Christian religion should always be expressed in plain and
simple language, avoiding all floweriness, and allegorical or

metaphorical images intended to express spiritual truths should not be dragged from the Bible and then interpreted with a grotesque literalness. 'In the New Testament', he writes in *The Uncommercial Traveller* ('Two Views of a Cheap Theatre'), 'there is the most beautiful and affecting history conceivable by man, and there are terse models for all prayer and for all preaching'. In the case of religious discourse addressed to children it was particularly important to use simple and straightforward language and the style of his secular *Child's History* of England, full of characteristically Dickensian imagery and wit, contrasts strikingly with the deliberately plain somewhat fairy-tale, style he adopted to write a life of Jesus for his children in the late 1840s.

This life of Jesus, based mainly on the Gospels of Matthew and Luke, was not intended for publication by Dickens and was not, in fact, published until 1934 under the title *The Life of Our Lord*. In it Christ is presented as an infinitely compassionate teacher and healer, and especially concerned with children and the poor. There is no reference to the doctrine of the Trinity or to the Virgin Birth; Dickens writes simply, 'His father's name was Joseph, and his mother's name was Mary'. An angel, 'all light and beautiful' moves over the grass towards the shepherds to tell them

> There is a child born today in the City of Bethlehem near here, who will grow up to be so good that God will love him as his own son; and he will teach men to love one another, and not to quarrel and hurt one another; and his name will be Jesus Christ; and people will put that name in their prayers, because they will know that God loves it, and will know that they should love it too.

When he comes to relate the miracles performed by Christ he defines the word 'miracle' as meaning 'something very wonderful and which could not be done without God's leave and assistance'. It is because Christ is so good that God gives him the power to work miracles. Allowing for the fact that the narrative is written for children so that it would be inappropriate to introduce such mysteries as the doctrine of the Trinity, one can still see that it is the humanity and not the divinity of Christ, his acts of mercy and charity rather than his ordaining of the Sacraments, that is all-important for Dickens. During the same time he was writing his 'Children's New Testament' (his own title for the book) Dickens was working on *Dombey and Son* and it is interesting to note how close is his account of Jesus in the children's book to the description of Christ's Ministry that appears in that novel:

> The blessed history, in which the blind lame palsied beggar, the criminal, the woman stained with shame, the shunned of all our dainty clay, has each a portion … the ministry of Him who, through the round of human life, and all its hopes and griefs, from birth to death, from infancy to age, had sweet compassion for, and interest in, its every scene and stage, its every suffering and sorrow. (*DS*, 58)

It was at this time also that Dickens, increasingly irritated by the way in which sectarian squabbles in the Church of England were preventing progress in the matter of public education, became for a few years a member of the congregation attending the Rev. Edward Tagart's Unitarian Chapel in Little Portland Street (during his visit to Boston in 1842 he had been deeply impressed by the preaching of the great Unitarian pastor William Ellery Channing). Clearly, the Unitarian rejection of the doctrine of the Trinity and the Divinity of Christ would have been congenial to him at this time and Tagart became a personal friend. Dickens composed an elaborate inscription for engraving on a silver salver presented to Tagart by his flock and referred in it to the minister's 'labours in the cause of that religion which has sympathy for men of every creed and ventures to pass judgement on none'. In the event, his friendship with Tagart proved more long-lasting than Dickens's official Unitarianism. As already noted, the growth of the Broad Church movement in the Church of England facilitated his return to Anglicanism and even, eventually, to the appearance of wholly admirable Anglican clergymen in his novels (The Rev. Frank Milvey in *Our Mutual Friend* and that sprightly young 'muscular Christian', the Rev. Septimus Crisparkle in *Drood*).

Dickens's faith seems not to have been shaken by the great Science v. Religion debate that was so much a feature of the intellectual life of his day, having a strong belief in Nature as the Book of God in which geologists, chemists, physicists and other scientists gradually learn to read more and more. His ideal engineer and inventor Daniel Doyce

... never said, I discovered this adaptation or invented that combination; but showed the whole thing as if the Divine artificer had made it, and he had happened to find it. So modest was he about it, such a pleasant touch of respect was mingled with his quiet admiration of it, and so calmly convinced he was that it was established on irrefragable laws. (*LD*, II. 8)

Writing a few years later to his Swiss friend de Cerjat about the uproar surrounding the publication of *Essays and Reviews* (1860), a volume in which a group of Broad Church clergymen attacked Biblical literalism and showed openness towards scientific discoveries, Dickens said he understood the position of the writers to be

... that certain parts of the Old Testament have done their intended function in the education of the world *as it was*; but that mankind, like the individual man, is designed by the Almighty to have an infancy and a maturity, and that, as it advances, the machinery of its education must advance too …. The science of geology is quite as much a revelation to man as books of an immense age and of (at the best) doubtful origin.

He is, in fact, placing many of the stories of the Old Testament on the same level as the myths and legends of ancient Greece as discussed by him in his 1848 review of Robert Hunt's *The Poetry of Science* (see above, p. 20). He goes on:

… the Church should not gradually shock and lose the more thoughtful and logical of human minds; but should be so gently and considerately yielding as to retain them, and, through them, hundreds of thousands … . What these bishops and such-like say about revelation, in assuming it to be finished and done with, I can't in the least understand. Nothing is discovered without God's intention and assistance, and I suppose every new knowledge of His works that is conceded to man to be distinctly a revelation by which men are to guide themselves. (21 May 1863)

He returns to the subject in a speech to the Birmingham and Midland Institute in 1869, ridiculing the charge that a 'material age' must be 'an irreligious age':

… has electricity become more material in the mind of any sane, or moderately insane [*laughter*] man, woman or child, because of the discovery that in the good providence of God it was made available for the service and use of man to an immeasurably greater extent than for his destruction? Do I make a more material journey to the bedside of my dying parents or my dying child when I travel there at the rate of sixty miles an hour, than when

I travel thither at the rate of six? Rather, in the swift case, does not my agonized heart become overfraught with gratitude to that Supreme Beneficence from whom alone can have proceeded the wonderful means of shortening my suspense?

No comment by Dickens on Darwin, the scientist whose work posed the severest test for Victorian believers, has come down to us. It is probable that he at least looked into the copy of *The Origin of Species* that he had in his library, but certain that he would have read and approved the long, lucid, and highly respectful, article on the *Origin*, entitled 'Natural Selection', published in *All The Year Round* on 7 July 1860. This goes into considerable detail about Darwin's theory

... that, probably, all the organic beings which have ever lived on this earth have descended from some one primordial form, into which life was first breathed by the Creator.

Thinking back to Chapter 4 above may help us to see Dickens might well have found reassurance (and encouragement to accept Darwinism) in the proposition that 'as Natural Selection works solely by and for the good of each being, all corporeal and mental endowments will tend to progress towards perfection'. And the mockery of 'timid persons, who purposely cultivate a certain inertia of minds, and who love to cling to their preconceived ideas' as well as the expressions of pride and satisfaction that Darwin should live in an age and a country where such theories as his can be propounded without fears of 'the rack and the stake' read as though they could well have been interpolations by Dickens himself (the identity of the writer of the article has yet to be discovered).

Before closing this chapter we should turn from difficulties encountered by Christian believers in the 19th century as a result of living in an age of such great scientific advances to more perennial religious concerns, and briefly consider Dickens's attitude towards the Four Last Things – Death, Judgment, Heaven and Hell. The most famous death in Dickens is, of course, Little Nell's and it is following that that we find one of his earliest and most elaborate statements of what he calls 'a mighty, universal Truth':

> When Death strikes down the innocent and young, for every fragile form from which he has let the panting spirit free, a hundred virtues rise, in shapes of mercy, to walk the world and bless it. Of every tear that sorrowing mortals shed on such green graves, some good is born, some gentler nature comes. In the Destroyer's steps there spring up bright creations that defy his power, and his dark path becomes a way of light to Heaven. (*OCS*, 72)

In his own personal life he felt that the spirit of the dead Mary Hogarth continued to guide and inspire him. In the 'best aspects' of the tremendous welcome he received in America in 1842, he felt, he wrote to Forster, 'the presence and influence of that spirit which directs my life, and through a heavy sorrow has pointed upward with unchanging finger for more than four years past'. He touches again on the special immortality of the good (this time those who died old) in the *Carol* when Scrooge is shown the terrible vision of what his deathbed will be if he persists in his grasping miserhood:

> Oh cold, cold, rigid dreadful Death, set up thine altar here, and dress it with such terrors as thou hast at thy command: for this is thy dominion! But of the loved, revered, and honoured head, thou canst not turn one hair to thy dread purposes, or make one feature odious. It is not that the hand is heavy and will fall down when released; it is not that the heart and pulse are still; but that

the hand WAS open, generous, and true; the heart brave,
warm, and tender; and the pulse a man's. Strike, Shadow,
strike! And see his good deeds springing from the wound,
to sow the world with life immortal!

Dickens may or may not have believed in the resurrection of
the body or reunion with loved ones after death (in a letter of
condolence [31 Jan. 1849] to his widowed brother-in-law
Henry Burnett on the death of a little son, Dickens says only
that 'we *may* believe' [my italics] that the child has in 'that
enduring world … rejoined his mother') but he certainly held
always to the belief that the good achieved *some* form of
immortality. Again, we cannot tell whether he really believed
that they literally became angels, or whether he uses the term
simply as a metaphor (even on the tombstone of Mary Hogarth
– 'Young, beautiful and good, God in his mercy numbered her
with his angels at the early age of seventeen') to express their
continued existence in some other dimension or in the effect of
their lives on those still living. At no stage of his life, one
imagines, did he spend much time thinking about the next
world, being so wholly focused on this one where, if only all
Christian people could be made truly aware of the pernicious,
soul-destroying squalor and misery in which the masses are
condemned to live

> … men, delayed no more by stumbling-blocks of their
> own making, which are but specks of dust upon the path
> between them and eternity, would then apply themselves,
> like creatures of one common origin, owing one duty to
> the Father of one family, and tending to one common end,
> to make the world a better place! (*DS*, 47)

Nor is there much evidence that Dickens spent much time
brooding over the problem of evil. That evil existed and could
exist in human form he had no doubt. It could also inhere in

corrupted man-made institutions like Chancery ('most pestilent of hoary sinners') in *Bleak House* and the Circumlocution Office in *Little Dorrit*. As regards individuals, he feared, he said in his preface to *Oliver Twist* with reference to Sikes, that 'there are in the world some insensible and callous natures that do become, at last, utterly and irredeemably bad' but, interestingly, makes no mention of Fagin, who undoubtedly came from very deep within Dickens's psyche, representing and embodying an apprehension of evil that went far beyond the brutality of Sikes, and surprising even his creator (he was, Dickens wrote to Forster, 'such an out-and-outer I don't know what to make of him'). By comparison with Fagin, Dickens's other devil-figure, Rigaud/Blandois in *Little Dorrit*, seems a much more conventional Mephistophelean creation (see also above, p. 147) but serves to dramatise Dickens's belief by this time that there were people in the world whom no amount of 'philosophical philanthropy' (which might have found some mitigating circumstances, such as the environment in which he was brought up, in the case of Sikes) could explain away. 'I tell you this, my friend, ' says the landlady of the Break of Day in *Little Dorrit*, to a customer who has been advocating a philosophically philanthropic view of a wife-murderer (Blandois, in fact):

> That there are people (men and women both, unfortunately) who have no good in them — none. That these are people whom it is necessary to detest without compromise. That there are people who must be dealt with as enemies of the human race. That there are people who have no human heart, and who must be crushed like savage beasts and cleared out of the way. They are but few, I hope; but I have seen (in this world here where I find myself, and even at the little Break of Day) that there are such people. (*LD*, I. 11)

'Crushed.' This is just what happens to Rigaud who is crushed by the collapse of the Clennam house, and indeed most of Dickens's evil characters meet a violent end (with the notable exception of the great hypocrites — Pecksniff, Heep, Littimer, Skimpole — who can always continue to batten on society in one way or another), as will be the fate of corrupted institutions like the *ancien régime* in the France of *A Tale of Two Cities* (the death of Krook the 'Lord Chancellor' by spontaneous combustion in *Bleak House* prefigures, we are told, what will happen to the real Court of Chancery and 'all authorities in all places ... where false pretences are made, and where injustice is done'). There is a horrific finality about their deaths which suggests annihilation, and with it the negation of all the evil they have perpetrated.* Dickens seems to reverse the sense of Shakespeare's Mark Antony's famous lines about the evil that men do living after them and the good being 'oft interred with their bones' when, after noting in *Our Mutual Friend* (I. 9), how the Boffins' natural goodness had survived unscathed all their years of servitude under the monstrous old miser Harmon, he comments

And this is the eternal law. For, evil often stops short at itself and dies with the doer of it; but Good, never.

As to beliefs about Hell and eternal punishment, Dickens, like so many Victorians, seems to have found them both morally offensive and somewhat ludicrous (one thinks of the painting he notices in a Roman church showing 'a select party of souls, frying') and to have leant — maybe not very consciously — more towards something like the contemporary theological concept of 'annihilationism' (interestingly discussed in relation to *Our Mutual Friend* by Michael Wheeler in

---

* (Steerforth in *David Copperfield*, Dickens's tragic villain, is a notable exception here; he is drowned in the great tempest but David always remembers him for all his fine qualities and cherishes his memory.

his *Death and the Future Life in Victorian Literature and Theology*, 1990).

*

In the end, however, it does not seem very profitable to try pinning Dickens down to any specific beliefs about the after-life. His extreme hostility, manifested in a number of fiercely satirical articles, towards one group of people who were very much preoccupied with the subject, the Spiritualist 'rappers', can, I think, be related to his strong belief, documented in this chapter, that we should as Christians be concerning ourselves with doing good in this world rather than trying to peer into the next. Nor, though his stories, especially the Christmas Books and Stories and the later novels, are permeated with motifs of resurrection, rebirth ('change of heart') and redemption and are deeply Christian in feeling, is it profitable to try and extract from them any system of theological belief. Rather, therefore, than attempting any summing-up of Dickens's religious posi-tion, it seems better to end with a piece of Christmas writing, less familiar, perhaps, than Pickwickian festivities at Dingley Dell or the *Christmas Carol* but one that seems to me to be instinct with so much that Christianity essentially meant to Dickens. It comes from the end of his Special Christmas Num-ber of *Household Words* for 1854, 'The Seven Poor Travellers':

> Going through the woods, the softness of my tread upon the mossy ground and among the brown leaves, enhanced the Christmas sacredness by which I felt surrounded. As the whitened stems environed me, I thought how the Founder of the time had never raised his benignant hand, save to bless and heal, except in the case of one uncon-scious tree. By Cobham Hall, I came to the village, and the churchyard where the dead had been quietly buried,

'in the sure and certain hope' which Christmas-time inspired. What children could I see at play, and not be loving of, recalling who had loved them! No garden that I passed was out of unison with the day, for I remembered that the tomb was in a garden, and that 'she, supposing him to be the gardener', had said, 'Sir, if thou have born him hence, tell me where thou hast laid him and I will take him away'. In time, the distant river with the ships came full in view, and with it pictures of the poor fishermen, mending their nets, who arose and followed him — of the teaching of the people from a ship pushed off a little way from shore, by reason of the multitude — of a majestic figure walking on the water, in the loneliness of night. My very shadow on the ground was eloquent of Christmas; for did not the people lay their sick where the mere shadows of the men who had heard and seen him might fall as they passed along?

List of Abbreviations

All quotations from Dickens's letters, other than those included in Forster, are taken from the volumes of the Pilgrim Edition of the *Letters of Charles Dickens*, ed. G. Storey, M. House et al., Oxford,

1965: if after 1864 from *The Letters of Charles Dickens*, ed. Walter Dexter, 1938. All quotations from Dickens's speeches are taken from *The Speeches from Charles Dickens*, ed. K.J. Fielding, Oxford, 1960.

Further Reading

Included below are scholarly works referred to in the text where bibliographical details are not provided there; studies particularly relevant to the topics discussed in this book; a selection of standard works on special aspects of Dickens's life and work; and major reference works.

Ackroyd, Peter — *Dickens* (1990)

Andrews, Malcolm — *Dickens and the Grown-up Child* (1994)

Andrews, Malcolm — *Dickens on England and the English* (1979)

Armstrong, Frances — *Dickens and the Concept of Home* (1990)

Carey, John — *The Violent Effigy. A Study of Dickens' Imagination* (2nd. ed., (1979)

Chesterton, G.K. — *Dickens* (1906)

Chittick, Kathryn — *Dickens and the 1830s* (1990)

Collins, Philip — *Dickens and Crime* (rev. ed., 1963)

Collins, Philip — *Dickens and Education* (rev. ed., 1964)

Higbie, Robert — *Dickens and Imagination* (1998)

House, Humphry — *The Dickens World* (rev. ed., 1942)

Johnson, Edgar — *Charles Dickens. His Tragedy and Triumph* (rev. ed., 1977)

Meckier, Jerome — *Innocent Abroad: Charles Dickens's American Engagements* (1990)

Newsom, Robert — *Dickens on the Romantic Side of Familiar Things. BLEAK HOUSE and the Novel Tradition* (1977)

Orwell, George — 'Charles Dickens' (in *Inside the Whale and Other Essays*, 1940)

Patten, Robert — *Charles Dickens and His Publishers* (1978)

Pope, Norris — *Dickens and Charity* (1978)

Sanders, Andrew — *Charles Dickens, Resurrectionist* (1982)

Schlicke, Paul — *Dickens and Popular Entertainment* (1985)

Schlicke, Paul (ed.)	*The Oxford Reader's Companion to Dickens* (1999)
Slater, Michael	*Dickens on America and the Americans* (1979)
Slater, Michael	*Dickens and Women* (rev. ed. 1986)
Smith, Grahame	*Dickens. A Literary Life* (1996)
Stewart, Garrett	*Dickens and the Trials of Imagination* (1974)
Stone, Harry	*Dickens and the Invisible World; fairy tales, fantasy and fabling* (1980)
Tomalin, Claire	*Invisible Woman. The Story of Nelly Ternan and Charles Dickens* (Penguin ed., 1991)
Trilling, Lionel	'Little Dorrit' (in his *The Opposing Self*, 1955)
Walder, Dennis	*Dickens and Religion* (1981)
Welsh, Alexander	*The City of Dickens* (1971)
Wilson, Angus	*The World of Charles Dickens* (1970)

Dickens's essays and journalistic pieces for *The Examiner* and *Household Words* referred to in this book may be conveniently found in the Dent Uniform Edition of Dickens's Journalism, ed. Michael Slater, vol.2, *The Amusements of the People; reports, essays and reviews 1834-1851* (1996) and vol.3, *'Gone Astray' and other papers from HOUSEHOLD WORDS 1851-1859* (1998). The most comprehensive edition of Dickens's work currently available is the Everyman Dickens (Everyman Paperbacks, Orion Publishing Group).

Index

Diary of a Man in Despair

Friedrich Reck-Malleczewen   £6.99 Paperback   0 7156 3100 4

A forgotten literary masterpiece by a Prussian aristocrat whose fascinating journal and indictment of Hitler's regime, written between 1936 and 1944, has astonished and delighted readers and critics alike.

'very, very rarely one comes across a book so remarkable and so unexpectedly convincing that it deserves more to be quoted than to be reviewed ...I beg you to read this bitterly courageous book'   Frederic Raphael, *The Sunday Times*

'a vivid and extremely personal evocation of the Nazi era – a small masterpiece'   Ben Rogers, *Financial Times*

'an indisputable humanist masterpiece'
                                        Walter Ellis, *The Times*

Cleopatra's Wedding Present
Travels through Syria
Robert Tewdwr Moss   £6.99 Paperback   0 7156 3099 7

Robert Tewdwr Moss describes his travel experiences with rare charm and aplomb.

'it would be hard to find a more archly entertaining, slyly informative, or poignant travel book than this'
                                        Philip Hoare, *Independent*

'Tewdwr Moss's intense, evocative account of his travels through Syria is a perfect book of its kind. Its author demonstrates intelligence, curiosity, humour, compassion, and commendable powers of observation: everything that is required of a travel writer'
                                Lucretia Stewart, *Times Literary Supplement*

The Way of Hermes

Translated by Clement Salaman, Dorine van Oyen, William D. Wharton, Jean-Pierre Mahé . £6.99 Paperback 0 7156 3093 8

The *Corpus Hermeticum* is a collection of short philosophical treatises, a powerful fusion of Greek and Egyptian thought, written in Greek in Alexandria between the first and third centuries AD. They are still read as inspirational spiritual writings today.

These translations of Hermetic writings and aphorisms provide both general reader and scholar with new English versions, based on reliable texts and faithful to the spirit and beauty of the original.

One Woman's War

Eve-Ann Prentice   £6.99 Paperback   0 7156 3104 7

A personal account of the war in the Balkans by a senior *Times* journalist, hailed by Harold Pinter as 'a powerful and important book'.

'*One Woman's War*, spurred by the death of the author's Serb interpreter during the Nato bombing of Kosovo, is an unselfconscious, intensely human and exceptionally honest reflection of the past ten years of conflict'

Allan Mallinson, *The Times*

'makes the valid point that the foreign press engaged in dangerous "demonisation" of the Serbs'

Peter Millar, *The Sunday Times*

'in the best tradition of a rare kind of eyewitness war reporting, the sort that is highly readable, but does nothing to make the military theatre an inviting destination'

Elaine Lafferty, *Irish Times*

The Pig: A British History
Julian Wiseman   £6.99 Paperback   0 7156 3092 X

A history of one of Britain's best-loved creatures, including the development of its husbandry.

'elegantly slender ... full of delightful pictures of the different breeds. Gripping'   *Independent*

'brings home to one what splendid creatures pigs are and what a contribution they have made to good living and even to survival'   Lord Blake, *Financial Times*

'a fine and well-told morality tale, whose basic message applies not only to pigs but to all livestock in all ages, the world over'   Colin Tudge, *New Scientist*

White Stains
Aleister Crowley   £6.99 Paperback   0 7156 3103 9

Branded 'the most terrible man in England' in the 1920s, Aleister Crowley enjoyed a measure of notoriety in his lifetime that few would be able to match. *White Stains*, a collection of Crowley's poetry praised by W.B. Yeats, published in paperback for the first time, has been called 'the filthiest book of verse ever written' and of the first edition of 100 numbered copies, 83 were pulped and burned by Her Majesty's Customs in 1924.

This edition includes an introduction by John Symonds, Crowley's literary executor and biographer.

An Intelligent Person's Guide to Ethics
Mary Warnock   £6.99 Paperback   0 7156 3089 X

'one of the best guides to ethics available'
Ray Monk, *Sunday Telegraph*

'this admirable book fully lives up to its title'
Robert Grant, *The Times*

An Intelligent Person's Guide to History
John Vincent   £6.99 Paperback   0 7156 3090 3

'not only is Vincent one of the great historians of 19th-century British politics, he is also that rarest of things in academic history: a witty prose stylist'

Niall Ferguson, *Daily Telegraph*

An Intelligent Person's Guide to Modern Ireland
John Waters   £6.99 Paperback   0 7156 3091 1

'John Waters skilfully attacks those who decry any sense of nationalism or belittle any aspiration that the two parts of Ireland should be united'

Michael O'Toole, *Irish News* (Belfast)

Boogie-Woogie
Danny Moynihan   £5.99 Paperback   0 7156 3102 0

Much-praised hilarious satire of the incestuous world of New York's contemporary art scene.

'Moynihan's first novel is spectacular stuff'

Harriet Lane, *Observer*

'a filthy corker of a book'   Jilly Cooper

'subversive, darkly funny'   *The Times*

'a highly amusing first novel'   *Tatler*

'witty satire... an excellent first novel'   *Daily Mail*

Intimate Cartographies
Lynne Alexander   £5.99 Paperback   0 7156 3095 4

A beautifully-constructed tale of a mapmaker who comes to terms with loss through the discipline of her work.

'Alexander has chosen the most difficult of subjects, the death of a child. She has treated it with sensitivity and wit, manic levity and the utmost respect, and has created something quite haunting'   Carol Birch, *Independent*

Too Fast To Live
Bidisha   £5.99 Paperback   0 7156 3098 9

A modern-day story of misdirected passions and amoral ambitions in a subversive rewriting of the Arthurian saga.

'Bidisha is clearly a dazzlingly creative writer'
     Anthea Lawson, *The Times*

'a dark violent tale that gets under your nails like the London grime it describes'   Francesca Gavin, *Dazed and Confused*

'an inventive addition to the current school of cockney cool'
     Independent on Sunday

Charlotte
The Final Journey of Jane Eyre
D.M. Thomas   £5.99 Paperback   0 7156 3094 6

An extraordinary, imaginative deconstruction of Charlotte Brontë's *Jane Eyre*, set partly in modern-day Martinique.

'a wickedly irreverent antidote to earnest study'
     Charlotte Cory, *Independent*

'the test of a text like this is whether you can put it down. I couldn't. I hurtled on, gripped by the simplest desire any reader ever has. I wanted to find out what happened'
     Patricia Duncker, *New Statesman*

Never Trust A Rabbit

Jeremy Dyson £5.99 Paperback 0 7156 3097 0

Twelve enchantingly surreal stories, recently serialised on BBC Radio Four, by Jeremy Dyson, one of *The League of Gentlemen*.

'*Never Trust a Rabbit* is ...expertly told and structured, being filled with such utterly surreal and fantastic twists and turns as one might expect of a member of BBC2's *The League of Gentlemen*'

Dominic Bradbury, *Times Metro*

'A stunning debut. His stories nestle in the little chink between Roald Dahl and Borges'

Adam Mars-Jones, *Observer*

Layer Cake

J.J. Connolly £5.99 Paperback 0 7156 3096 2

The critically-acclaimed contemporary gangland thriller set in London's underworld, described by Bruce Reynolds as 'the best crime novel I've ever read'.

'*Layer Cake* is a storming piece of work, funny and serious by turns with an abiding sense of conviction'

Guardian

'this year's crime read should be J.J. Connolly's *Layer Cake*'
Mike Pattenden, *Times Metro*

'mission accomplished. One novel in and Connolly has hit the jackpot'

*****, *Uncut*

www.ducknet.co.uk

ORDER FORM (BLOCK CAPITALS PLEASE)

SURNAME _____ FIRST NAME _____

ADDRESS _____

_____

_____ POSTCODE _____

METHOD OF PAYMENT (PLEASE TICK AS APPROPRIATE)

☐ Invoice to my Grantham Book Services account
☐ By cheque (payable to Duckworth Publishers)
☐ Please send account opening details (trade customers only)
☐ By credit card (Access/ Visa / Mastercard / Amex)

Card no: ☐ ☐ ☐ ☐ ☐ ☐ ☐ ☐ ☐ ☐ ☐ ☐ ☐ ☐ ☐ ☐ ☐ ☐ ☐

Expiry date: ___ / ___ / ___   Authorising Signature: _____

POSTAGE (Private customers) Please note that the following postage and packing charges should be added to your order:

UK deliveries: £3 on orders up to £16; £4 on orders over £16
Export surface: £3.50 for first book + £0.50 for each additional book
Export airmail: £7 for the first book + £2 for each additional book

QTY	ISBN	TITLE	PRICE	TOTAL
_____	0 7156 3102 0	Boogie-Woogie	£5.99	_____
_____	0 7156 3094 6	Charlotte	£5.99	_____
_____	0 7156 3099 7	Cleopatra's Wedding Present	£6.99	_____
_____	0 7156 3100 4	Diary of a Man in Despair	£6.99	_____
_____	0 7156 3095 4	Intimate Cartographies	£5.99	_____
_____	0 7156 3088 1	IPG to Dickens	£6.99	_____
_____	0 7156 3089 X	IPG to Ethics	£6.99	_____
_____	0 7156 3090 3	IPG to History	£6.99	_____
_____	0 7156 3091 1	IPG to Modern Ireland	£6.99	_____
_____	0 7156 3096 2	Layer Cake	£5.99	_____
_____	0 7156 3097 0	Never Trust a Rabbit	£5.99	_____
_____	0 7156 3104 7	One Woman's War	£6.99	_____
_____	0 7156 3092 X	The Pig: A British History	£6.99	_____
_____	0 7156 3098 9	Too Fast to Live	£5.99	_____
_____	0 7156 3093 8	The Way of Hermes	£6.99	_____
_____	0 7156 3103 9	White Stains	£6.99	_____
			TOTAL £	_____

To: Sales Dept, Duckworth, 61 Frith Street, London W1D 3JL
Tel:+44 (0) 20 7434 4242 Fax: +44 (0) 20 7434 4420
Heidi@duckworth-publishers.co.uk